T0339693

The Spartan W@rker

The field of Organizational Psychology and Occupational Stress is complex and multifaceted. Many efforts have been made by several authors to write books that would have assisted employees in becoming more satisfied, relaxed and thus happier with their work, but such a result seems difficult and complicated to achieve.

In *The Spartan W@rker*, the authors approach the research of Organizational Psychology and Occupational Stress from a fresh and different perspective. It compares the modern work environment with the features and way of life of the famous Greek Spartan warriors. Spartan warriors embraced a unique lifestyle which made them become more resilient, engaged, committed and efficient in their everyday lives, both in times of peace and war. The book proposes that in an increasingly demanding work environment, such an approach would be very beneficial for workers who want and need to learn how to become more resilient and thus remain unaffected from the daily stresses of modern life. This book dedicates itself to explaining in detail the mechanisms through which occupational stress negatively affects our lives as well as in proposing techniques that will help individuals to enhance their coping skills in dealing with stress.

This book will appeal to a broad range of professionals looking to understand and reduce the occurrence of occupational stress with its playful style, which is nevertheless grounded in scientific literature and research.

Konstantinos Perrotis is an Organizational Psychologist and Business Consultant. He holds a bachelor's degree in Psychology and Business Management with High Distinctions, from the American University of Greece, Deree. He was awarded his PhD by Lancaster University, with a thesis on Organizational Health and Wellbeing. Dr. Perrotis acts as a Business Psychology consultant for a number of companies on matters of Recruitment, Human Resources Management, Occupational Stress, Productivity, Leadership, Motivation and other relevant topics.

Cary L. Cooper is the 50th Anniversary Professor of Organizational Psychology and Health at Manchester Business School, University of Manchester. He is the President of the CIPD, President of the British Academy of Management, President of RELATE and President of the Institute of Welfare. He was knighted by the Queen in 2014 for his contribution to the social sciences.

Routledge Focus on Business and Management

The fields of business and management have grown exponentially as areas of research and education. This growth presents challenges for readers trying to keep up with the latest important insights. Routledge Focus on Business and Management presents small books on big topics and how they intersect with the world of business.

Individually, each title in the series provides coverage of a key academic topic, whilst collectively, the series forms a comprehensive collection across the business disciplines.

Understanding the Born Global Firm
Neri Karra

The Internet of Things and Business
Martin De Saulles

The Search for Entrepreneurship
Simon Bridge

Neurobusiness
Stephen Rhys Thomas

Auditing Teams: Dynamics and Efficiency
Mara Cameran, Angelo Ditillo and Angela Pettinicchio

The Reflective Entrepreneur
Dimo Dimov

The Spartan W@rker
Konstantinos Perrotis and Cary L. Cooper

The Spartan W@rker

**Konstantinos Perrotis
and Cary L. Cooper**

LONDON AND NEW YORK

First published 2018
by Routledge
2 Park Square, Milton Park, Abingdon, Oxon OX14 4RN

and by Routledge
605 Third Avenue, New York, NY 10017

First issued in paperback 2021

Routledge is an imprint of the Taylor & Francis Group, an informa business

British Library Cataloguing-in-Publication Data
A catalogue record for this book is available from the British Library

Library of Congress Cataloging-in-Publication Data
A catalog record for this book has been requested

ISBN 13: 978-1-03-209687-2 (pbk)
ISBN 13: 978-1-138-05958-0 (hbk)

Typeset in Times New Roman
by Apex CoVantage, LLC

Contents

Illustrations

Figures

Tables

Acknowledgements

I dedicate this book in the memory of my father, Theodoros G. Perrotis, who has enriched me with noble values and a strong personality from my adolescent years and whose example I have followed ever since in all aspects of my life.

In addition, I would like to thank my beloved wife and colleague, Mina Kantarou, psychologist, who has inspired me and supported me throughout the process of writing this book and in life overall. Finally, I would like to thank my mother, Zografia, and my brother, George, for their love and encouragement, and for always being there.

Introduction

The Spartan W@rker is not a usual book when it comes to discussing topics such as stress and resilience. It is a book based on historical data and scientific literature that aims to help you lead a healthier and more fulfilling life. Who would say no to that?

Before we begin, keep in mind that throughout the book a number of parallelisms will be made between the modern work environment and the ancient Spartan lifestyle in an effort to explain and relate certain topics as we move forward in the book.

We found writing this book exhilarating! Exhilarating due to the fact that it blends all of our knowledge on stress and resilience with the roots of Greek ancient history 2,500 years ago, where all philosophical and psychological knowledge originated.

So, you may choose this book because you are interested in stress in general, or because you want to reduce stress levels at work, or because you are just intrigued by the famous Spartans and how they managed to be highly resilient in such difficult and demanding times. Finally, it may be that you wish to find a sense of peace and satisfaction in your everyday life, regardless of the circumstances that each one has to deal with, whether you are facing a pleasant or an unpleasant day.

Well, no matter what your incentive will be, you have made a good choice because this book can work as a game changer for you!

Now, we would like to pose a dilemma:

Do you think that it is possible to lead a stress-free life in general? Do you believe that you can remain unaffected and preserve a sense of calmness, even when various hassles and stressful events are surrounding you? Just imagine that for a moment. You have woken up yet another Monday morning, and everything seems to go wrong. You did not hear the alarm, so you are rushing to get ready for work. You are driving, and you are stuck in traffic, most likely with other people who are experiencing something similar, rushing themselves throughout the day . . . And on top of that you start thinking of the important meeting that you will miss, what your colleagues will think about you and in general that your daily schedule has just imploded. Does this sound familiar? Does even reading such a story make you feel a little bit distressed?

Have you ever reached a point where you felt that you had no control over your mind and body? Having the feeling that the demands were over your ability to manage them? Well, if you respond positively to these questions, then you might have experienced increased levels of stress. At this point, a discussion regarding your experienced levels of stress during the past will be of minor importance, because at the end of our journey you will have become a Spartan warrior yourself (a metaphorical statement for increased competence to manage everyday stress), unaffected by stress and any daily hassle. Unaffected does not necessarily mean that you will not feel the stress and the discomfort that comes along with it, but it rather means that you will become more capable of dealing with it effectively through the new skills and coping techniques that this book will provide to you. After such knowledge you will only have to keep on enriching your coping abilities, and this will transform your quality of life in a positive way.

Throughout this book, you should keep in mind that feeling stressed is a normal condition that all human beings experience once in a while. It is a bodily and mental reaction through which your physical organism reacts and fights back in order to overcome any stressful and/or threatening situation. Stress can be our ally, always remember that! And even if it reaches disturbing levels, we have good news for you! There are a number of ways through which an individual can cope with stress, and this is what we are going to explore throughout the book.

The concept of the Spartan W@rker

The purpose of this book is to approach the research of Organizational Psychology and Occupational Stress from a different point of view. It links the modern work environment (which in the title – The Spartan W@rker – is metaphorically described as a war terrain with the use of the @ symbol) with the features and way of life of the famous Greek Spartan warriors. Spartan warriors had embraced a unique lifestyle which had enabled them to become more resilient, engaged, committed and efficient in their everyday lives, both in times of peace and war. So our book suggests that such an approach would be beneficial for modern workers who desire to learn new ways in order to become more resilient and thus to remain unaffected by daily hassles, especially in a constantly increasing, in terms of demands, work environment. But what exactly do we mean by the term 'resilience'?

According to Kobasa (1979): 'The construct of resilience refers to the ability of individuals to adapt successfully in the face of acute stress, trauma, or chronic adversity, maintaining or rapidly regaining psychological wellbeing and physiological homeostasis'. It is certainly the fact that the current work environment is so stressful as never before, and we are sure that such skills, if cultivated properly, could create more resilient workers who would eventually adopt a healthier lifestyle. High levels of resilience have been found to work as a shield against stress, thus protecting both the physical and psychological wellbeing of employees (Maddi & Khoshaba, 2005; Beddington, Cooper, Field, Goswami, Huppert, Jenkins, Jones, Kirkwood, Sahakian & Thomas, 2008; Robertson & Cooper, 2013).

This book dedicates itself to explaining in detail the mechanisms through which occupational stress negatively affects our lives as well as in proposing techniques that would help individuals to enhance their coping skills in dealing with stress. Furthermore, the chapters of this book are organized in such a way so as to introduce the topics of stress in a simplistic and playful manner, thus making the book friendlier to readers and making it easier for everyone to read it, regardless of the reader's occupational or academic background.

How will the book flow?

The book is divided in two parts, with the first one presenting the Spartan lifestyle and details about the Spartan warriors and also providing brief historical information related to the topic of stress. This will induct the readers to comprehend better the main concept of the book.

The second part of the book focuses mostly on the modern work environment and on the current situation regarding occupational stress as well as on the ways through which individuals can become Spartan W@rkers and thus more resilient to stress. In order to manage stress effectively, we must try not to reinvent the wheel but rather to look upon human history and to find examples of groups such as the Spartans who have managed to do so effectively. We can then use the characteristics of such a group and adjust them to the needs, demands, trends and requirements of modern society.

What can this book do for you?

This book will equip you with all the necessary knowledge concerning new skills and techniques that will help you to increase resilience and decrease stress both in your work and personal life. Such interventions against stress will:

- Improve your physical and psychological wellbeing, since training to develop personal resilience has been found to decrease stress levels and thus protect and improve general wellbeing (Robertson, Cooper, Sarkar & Curran, 2015).

- Boost your performance and productivity levels by developing concepts such as self-confidence, optimism, hope, positivism and personal insight (Luthans, Luthans & Luthans, 2004; Grant, Curtayne & Burton, 2009).
- Create better work–life balance by making you able to put forth challenging but manageable deadlines and effectively organize your workload, thus not carrying work back home (Lewis & Cooper, 2005; Cartwright & Cooper, 2009).
- Decrease levels of job insecurity through boosting your self-confidence, constantly enriching your skills and creating new job opportunities, thus becoming a necessity for the success of your company. This is really crucial, since job insecurity has been rated as one of the six most important work stressors that can negatively affect overall wellbeing (Industrial Society, 2001; De Witte, 2005).
- Enable you to create better work and personal relationships by actively seeking the benefits of support from others, interacting constructively on work matters and building true and meaningful connections with others. Such skills are also transferred to personal life, thus enriching the way we relate to loved ones too, dragging us away from feelings of isolation (Karasek, Triantis & Chaudhry, 1982; Cartwright & Cooper, 2009).
- Improve your levels of motivation by teaching you how to become more optimistic in life and to choose to see things from their positive aspect, thus recovering more quickly from setbacks and starting to take action towards goal completion (Seligman, 2011).
- Improve your levels of concentration and work engagement, so you find yourself being stimulated, being in a constant positive flow and focusing constructively on your work, where time passes without you even noticing, making work joyful and meaningful (Bakker & Demerouti, 2008; Robertson & Cooper, 2010).

References

Bakker, A. B., & Demerouti, E. (2008). Towards a Model of Work Engagement. *Career Development International*, 13, 209–223.

Beddington, J., Cooper, C. L., Field, J., Goswami, U., Huppert, F. A., Jenkins, R., Jones, H. S., Kirkwood, T. B., Sahakian, B. J., & Thomas, S. M. (2008). The Mental Wealth of Nations. *Nature*, 455, 1057–1060.

Cartwright, S., & Cooper, C. L. (2009). *The Oxford Handbook of Organisational Wellbeing*. Oxford: Oxford University Press.

de Witte, H. (2005). Job Insecurity: Review of the International Literature on Definitions, Prevalence, Antecedents and Consequences. *SA Journal of Industrial Psychology*, 31, 1–6.

Grant, A. M., Curtayne, L., & Burton, G. (2009). Executive Coaching Enhances Goal Attainment, Resilience and Workplace Well-Being: A Randomised Controlled Study. *The Journal of Positive Psychology*, 4, 396–407.

Industrial Society. (2001). Managing Best Practice. *Occupational Stress*, 83, 4–23.

Karasek, R. A., Triantis, K. P., & Chaudhry, S. S. (1982). Coworker and Supervisor Support as Moderators of Associations Between Task Characteristics and Mental Strain. *Journal of Organizational Behavior*, 3, 181–200.

Kobasa, S. C. (1979, January). Stressful Life Events, Personality, and Health: An Inquiry Into Hardiness. *Journal of Personality and Social Psychology*, 37.

Lewis, S., & Cooper, C. L. (2005). *Work-Life Integration: Case Studies of Organisational Change*. Hoboken, NJ: John Wiley and Sons, Ltd.

Luthans, F., Luthans, K. W., & Luthans, B. C. (2004). Positive Psychological Capital: Beyond Human and Social Capital. *Business Horizons*, 47, 45–50.

Maddi, S. R., & Khoshaba, D. M. (2005). *Resilience at Work: How to Succeed No Matter What Life Throws at You*. New York: Amacom.

Robertson, I. T., & Cooper, C. L. (2010). Full Engagement: The Integration of Employee Engagement and Psychological Well-Being. *Leadership & Organization Development Journal*, 31, 324–336.

Robertson, I. T., & Cooper, C. L. (2013). Resilience. *Stress and Health*, 29, 175–176.

Robertson, I. T., Cooper, C. L., Sarkar, M., & Curran, T. (2015). Resilience Training in the Workplace From 2003 to 2014: A Systematic Review. *Journal of Occupational and Organizational Psychology*, 88, 533–562.

Seligman, M. E. (2011). *Learned Optimism: How to Change Your Mind and Your Life*. New York: Vintage.

1 The philosophy of the Spartan lifestyle

Let us begin by introducing you to the philosophy behind the Spartan life-style. Which societal factors promoted such personality characteristics (i.e. persistence, self-confidence, self-efficacy, courage) that were in a way responsible for the resilient mentality of Spartans during turbulent and violent times? Sparta was considered a distinctive city-state of ancient Greece, located in the south area of Peloponnesus. Geographically rich and with a good climate, this region flourished around 750 BC. Spartans were well known as fierce warriors and for their military discipline, but also they were unique in terms of culture when compared to other Greek city-states and other nations of that time. Spartans were proud people, both for themselves and for their origins! Historical traces support that their ancestors arrived in the area during the Dorian invasion, and Spartans claimed that they were the 'Return of the Heraclids'. According to the Spartan poet Tyrtaeus, the Spartan kings were direct descendants of Hercules and asserted that their tribe had returned to Peloponnesus to continue their glorious legacy (Gerber, 1999). Their uniqueness stems from their persistence towards excellence and devotion to their state: excellence pertaining all activities they undertook, such as battle training, dancing, singing and athletic competition, and devotion to their state, undertaking a collectivist approach, with every Spartan being driven by motives of group cohesion and support towards others with a common goal – the wellbeing, prosperity and advancement of Sparta. For such reasons, Spartans had created a developmental/educational system (the Greek term is *agoge*) for all of Sparta's citizens (both male and female, although females followed a less demanding upbringing, but nevertheless demanding and radical when it comes to women concerning such an ancient period), with the aim to cultivate strong values, such as courage, pride, endurance, discipline and resilience. Behind the *agoge* training system lies a whole philosophy that was very futuristic and effective when taking into consideration that it existed approximately 2,500 years ago. The *agoge* system will be thoroughly analyzed in the next chapter, since it was considered as the backbone of ancient Sparta's fame, which involved the creation of the most elite warriors in ancient history.

In our times, those values still play a critical role in our lives and more specifically in our work lives. We are all striving for a successful and prosperous career in order to be financially free. To succeed at that, we need to be strong and determined towards our goals no matter the obstacles and difficulties we are going to meet along the way. In other terms, we need to be resilient and focused on the achievement of our goals no matter the stressors involved, and this is what you will achieve by implementing the techniques and advice provided in this book.

Spartans had a strict but at the same time fair law system where every political class had a voice. Spartans were really law-abiding citizens. They respected the laws (the Greek term is *eunomia*) developed by the famous legislator Lycurgus, since they believed that only within a just and fair environment was it possible for someone to find security and stability. At the same time, they had created a sophisticated governing system. To begin with, Spartans had two kings; in times of war, one led the army in the battlefield and the other remained behind to lead the city-state. Below them, hierarchically, there were 30 elected *ephoroi* as Spartans called them (in our times this could be paralleled with middle/upper management of a company). All of them were individuals over the age of 60 who were well respected by everyone, due to the fact that through the years they had cultivated leading wisdom, or in other terms their leadership skills, and had fought honourably in numerous battles. Interestingly, every year, five citizens were elected, for only once in their lifetime, to be members of the governmental scheme, and they represented the voice of the people. They had such a power that if they wanted, they could call even the king to a trial, if, let's say, corruption allegations existed (Cartledge, 2013). Such a structure was pretty just and created a sense of bonding between Spartans.

Women in Sparta

A characteristic that distinguished ancient Sparta from the other Greek city-states was that women had an active role in society. This is really spectacular! Sparta was the only Greek city-state and most probably one of the few regions in the ancient world where women were considered equal to men and had the right to vote and speak for themselves; they were highly respected by other members of society. It seems that the topic of gender inequality, which is still prominent in our modern societies, was nonexistent for Spartans, who believed that all human beings are equal between them regardless of their sex, thus promoting high commitment levels from all citizens to the state. Spartan women under this well-deserved equality excelled and were considered the most impressive in the ancient world (Pomeroy, 2002). Spartan women seemed to share the same lifestyle philosophy that modern women/business women seek. They were fit, took care of their appearance but without exaggeration, had a high self-esteem and confidence in their abilities and possessed very good interpersonal skills. It seems that both mental and physical ability were of high importance to those women, using them as a gauge of their self-worth. They were intellectual and motivated, and male Spartans always used to seek their advice in many topics. Although women did not follow the complete training program, in Greek named *agoge*, that male Spartans did, their training schedule was also demanding and stimulating both in physical and mental development. Instead of the rigorous physical training they were trained on dancing and choral work, and the majority of them were literate, self-confident and outspoken (Pomeroy, 2002). As Spartans believed, in order to give birth to a strong child and to provide the infant with a strong upbringing, both mentally and physically, the women had to be strong also in the same aspects, especially since the father was constantly away either at war or at training (Spartans were not allowed to live and sleep in their house, even if they were married, until their thirties).

All the aforementioned details regarding Spartan women in such an ancient era seem extraordinary even today! I am sure that the majority of the readers would think that the Spartans, with such a strong military structure, would have treated women in an inferior way. On the contrary, Spartans were proud of their women, and all Spartans, regardless of their sex, were constantly driven by an urge to improve themselves in every way and to reach perfection. Both male and female Spartans wanted to become citizens of a perfect city-state because, after all, a perfect nation or a perfect work environment is created by the quality of its human capital.

Spartan culture

Although Sparta showed some masterpieces of art and civilization, nevertheless it was more military oriented in order to be able to protect itself from the threats of that time period. Does this look familiar? Isn't it just like us today, as we are trying to protect ourselves from everyday demanding schedules and a 'to do' list that does not seem to reach an end?

So, Spartans invested not in the production of artefacts but rather to their personal development, since for them the most superior piece of art was nothing more than the strengthening of the self both physically and mentally.

A well-known Greek ancient saying – *nous igiis en somati igii* – denotes that a healthy mind exists in a healthy body. Consequently, when experiencing an internal balance, one can reach a level of homeostasis where peace, calmness and tranquillity occurs regardless of the external forces that one meets in everyday life, enabling a sense of physical and psychological wellbeing and enhanced levels of performance in everyday tasks (Cannon, 1935; Cartwright & Cooper, 2009; Chrousos, 2009). Spartans considered themselves as the most brilliant artefacts in terms of self-discipline, ethos, morality, respect, physical and psychological state, all features that imply a continuous training and effort that fostered them to become more resilient day by day no matter the obstacles met along the way.

Furthermore, in terms of arts, dancing and singing were considered important for Spartans (both for males and females), because through such activities they were enriching their spirit, they kept morale high and, indirectly, they were lowering their anxiety levels during stressful periods. Spartans used dance as a technique to empower their fighting skills during battle since they were well known for their choreographic battle moves. Basically, they used dance as a means to become trained and prepared for battle, uplifting their fighting/military performance to a higher level (Cartledge, 2013).

Spartans were considered minimalists both in their way of living and also in their sayings. They always preferred to be active listeners and to give short replies, but with higher meaning. Some very famous sayings that demonstrate Spartans' persistence and their willingness to live fully and with no fear are presented here (Plutarch & Talbert, 2005):

- King Leonidas's response to Persian Emperor Xerxes in the battle of Thermopylae, when he asked Spartans to lay down their weapons, was *molon labe*, meaning 'come and take them'. The Spartans were significantly outnumbered, but they resisted until the end, though they were all killed in battle.
- That saying comes in accordance with the Spartan mentality where, when a Spartan warrior was departing for a battle, his mother told him *i tan i epi tas* meaning that he should 'return with his shield or upon it', as a victor or dead.
- Finally, when King Philip of Macedonia sent some orders to Spartans, they laconically replied: 'What you wrote about, no.'

Concluding our introduction concerning the Spartan lifestyle, when referring to Sparta we can distinguish several commonalities with the modern society underlying various topics. The main differences simply reflect technological advancement. The human element remains the same, but in the majority of the cases, if we exclude university certificates and technical knowledge concerning any occupation, the inner self has been left unfulfilled. However, in our times a shift has been made again when business and life in general are under the microscope, in that companies constantly recruit individuals not only for their hard skills, which you can find in abundance, but for their soft skills that seem to play a critical role in the development of cohesive and bonded teams that can mix their talents and reach optimal performance (Zedeck & Goldstein, 2000).

In the next chapter we are going to complete our historical reference to ancient Spartans by giving extra notice to the system underlying the creation of Spartan warriors, to understand how these individuals were nurtured to become the most elite, fearless and fierce warriors of the ancient world.

References

Cannon, W. B. (1935). Stresses and Strain of Homeostasis. *The American Journal of the Medical Sciences*, 189, 1–14.

Cartledge, P. (2013). *Sparta and Lakonia: A Regional History 1300–362 BC*. Abingdon: Routledge.

Cartwright, S., & Cooper, C. L. (2009). *The Oxford Handbook of Organisational Wellbeing*. Oxford: Oxford University Press.

Chrousos, G. P. (2009). Stress and Disorders of the Stress System. *Nature Reviews Endocrinology*, 5, 374–381.

Gerber, D. E. (Ed.). (1999). Greek Elegiac Poetry: From the Seventh to the Fifth Centuries BC. *Cambridge, Massachusetts, London, England: The Loeb Classical Library*, 200, 258.

Plutarch, & Talbert, R. J. A. (2005). *On Sparta*. Rev. ed. New York: Penguin.

Pomeroy, S. B. (2002). *Spartan Women*. New York: Oxford University Press.

Zedeck, S., & Goldstein, I. L. (2000). The Relationship Between I/O Psychology and Public Policy: A Commentary. *Managing Selection in Changing Organizations: Human Resource Strategies*, 371–396.

2   The Spartan warrior

Are you prepared for a battle? You should be. . . . The modern work environment can be considered as a battle terrain where nothing is stable. If you want to reach the top tier of your craft, you need to fight your way up daily. You either fight or flee; you either persist or perish; you either believe in yourself/skills, keep your grounds and march forward or fall back to mediocrity.

In this chapter the famous concept of the Spartan warriors is going to be thoroughly analyzed, explaining the techniques that those individuals were using in order to deal with the demands of their everyday life, techniques that eventually led to the cultivation of a strong internal state of Spartan warriors, resulting in them becoming highly resilient against stress.

It is quite an oxymoron if you think about it: the fact that such a group of people in the south area of Greece, although moving against the cultural and political norms of all other Greeks and ancient civilization in general, had actually succeeded in developing and following such a distinct lifestyle, a lifestyle that equipped them not with luxurious and tangible assets but rather with intangible internal power and self-confidence that made them fierce even in the face of death. Such an assumption goes in accordance with specialists who state that Sparta was one of the most fascinating ancient societies that played a significant role in the development of the Western civilization (Cartledge, 2003). Although ancient Athens was famous for architectural monuments, democracy, philosophy and theatre, Sparta presented a matchless vigour when it comes to values such as duty, discipline and persistence. Such values reflect a societal/cultural cause worth dying for, a collectivist effort towards the common good of the state and a strong willingness to triumph in the face of overwhelming obstacles (Cartledge, 2003).

Thus, we believe that spending time exploring the way through which something like that was possible to succeed is worthwhile. We believe that we can relate the features of the Spartan lifestyle to our modern times and find commonalities that can help you lead a healthier and more fulfilling lifestyle. By doing so, we do not mean that you will have to embrace a harsh and demanding lifestyle and start going for survival exertions in the mountains (although this might be something that you as an individual might be fond of! It's up to you). On the other hand, we suggest that in order to become resilient and highly effective in your work environment, you need something more than just a seminar, a training course and a meeting with your colleagues or supervisor. You need something with a long-lasting effect. What you need in general terms is to evolve your physical and mental toughness. Mental toughness is considered by researchers as a critical feature that enables an individual to overcome successfully very demanding situations and perform to high standards, and it is suggested that it is an imperative characteristic for success in life (Jones & Moorhouse, 2007; Weinberg, 2010). Spartan warriors experienced substantially high levels of mental toughness.

However, in order to achieve such a transformation, you will have to change your way of thinking and change the way through which you see and perceive things – the way you behave. Changing your way of thinking is not an easy thing, though. Core beliefs cannot easily change. They can be altered, but they cannot completely change. Therefore, in order to achieve such a transformation, you will have to embrace new alternatives of thinking and challenging your beliefs, and this is how you can eventually change your behaviour. You must break yourself into pieces and reinvent yourself, as the military system does to Special Forces candidates during their induction training (Green, Emslie, O'Neill, Hunt & Walker, 2010). The military does so to its members and is highly successful; hence, something similar is needed in the business world, following an elegant, respectful and sophisticated way. Such a transformation, though, requires time and effort, since change does not come within a day and it is not always pleasant. It has both good and bad times. Keep this in mind as we proceed in this book.

The Spartans early on understood all the previously mentioned assumptions, and that is why they created an upbringing system called *agoge* (raising) that was implemented from childhood. Spartans were taken to military barracks from the age of 5, and they were obliged to live in the barracks until the age of 30, even if they were married. Spartans retired from the military around the age of 60. From the age of 5 they followed a harsh educational system that was highly demanding both physically and psychologically, with the aim of preparing them to defend their state. An upbringing system that was similar in many ways was also followed by female Spartans that involved both education and physical exercise. The influence that the females had in Spartan society also has been discussed in the previous chapter, and again it denotes the different mentality that Spartans had. They implemented their own methods and did not follow any system or any dicta-tion by the other Greek city-states. Women of course did not participate in battle, but they had to be physically fit for giving birth to a strong Spartan. Also women had to be strong (body and mind) in order to be socially active, to vote and state their opinion. It is really amazing that at that time no gender inequality was present and that all Spartans, regardless of their sex, were collectively working towards the common good of Sparta.

The aforementioned can be beautifully demonstrated by the sayings of a Spartan woman, Gorgo, wife of King Leonidas, who, when asked why Spartan women could be directive towards their men, replied that only Spar-tan women could give birth to real men, by being trained from birth to do so, and that is why they could also stand equal in front of men (Plutarch & Talbert, 2005).

Spartans had one main goal: To protect themselves from any harm. In order to achieve that they concluded that they had to become superior to others so no one could stand against them on the battlefield, and that is what they achieved for a prolonged period of time. They were striving for their survival, and in order to accomplish that they went to extremes, implement-ing harsh rules and procedures to prepare themselves. Selection of Spartans was made from birth, where the elders decided if the infant could be reared as a Spartan warrior or left to die in the Taygetos Mountains. The harsh upbringing started from the early years of life, where Spartans were left alone in the dark with limited nutrition in order to start becoming resilient against feelings of fear and exhaustion. As mentioned earlier, military train-ing started at the age of 5, and the first phase lasted for six years. Spartans were separated into teams and competed with other teams in a number of activities in order to cultivate a sense of belonging, trust and teamwork. Simultaneously, they were learning how to write and read and to dance while carrying weapons to enrich their battle movements. When Spartans reached the age of 12, extreme physical exercise was added in their training schedule. No matter the season (winter or summer), Spartan trainees wore only a cloak, with the objective to become resistant to adverse environ-mental conditions (i.e. heat and cold), and all their movements were done barefoot to toughen their feet. They were living in barracks following a sim-plistic lifestyle both in terms of the beds and the food they were consuming so as to be ready to face demanding conditions during battle in the future. Upon reaching the age of 18, Spartan trainees became trainers of younger Spartans for one year, and then, since they had reached adulthood, they were permitted to enter a Spartan mess as Spartan warriors. Each mess comprised 15 Spartan warriors of different years of age, and in this mess they were obliged to stay until the age of 30 even if they were married. Marriage was very important for Spartans, and if a Spartan was not married until the age of 30, then he was humiliated, since after all the most important thing in ancient Sparta was the upbringing of more elite warriors.

Spartans were in a constant effort to improve themselves through training in order to be ready for battle, since participating in a battle was what they were expecting, with pride. They even believed that dying in battle was the most noble death. As stated beautifully by Plutarch, Spartans were the only warriors who considered war as a positive break from their training for war. During war they wore a red cloak so as to cover their blood when they were wounded, and of course their slogan was 'bleed in training so as to avoid bleeding in war'. Spartans were warriors for their whole lives, and they were active in battles even after the age of 60.

What can be understood from all this is that a change of mentality and an increase in resilience levels cannot be done within a day and requires substantial and continuous effort. In order to become more resilient an individual must first have a sense of purpose. You need to know where you stand and where you want to go in life, to know your short-term goals and long-term objectives and to understand that in order to reach them you must transform yourself both mentally and physically into a whole new person, a new self. It is true that at the time you achieve a significant goal (e.g. complete a project, get a promotion, reach graduation) for which you have strived a lot, you are not the same person as the one who decided to achieve that goal in the first place. It is not the goal that you have achieved that is important here, but the person you have become along the way, surpassing every obstacle, meeting every deadline, dealing with people and managing your workload effectively. Through dealing with those things and by training and enriching yourself with adequate coping techniques, you become more resilient. It is important to keep in mind that you become more resilient through experience and through learning, so do not be afraid to face stressful situations. As Spartans did, you must face the demands and metaphorically bleed in everyday life so as to be ready and not bleed in the everyday battle for success. Deal with stressful situations and you will increase your self-confidence day by day, reaching your purpose and gradually becoming more resilient. Do not forget that this is the reason that you read this book: to become more resilient and stress free, to reach a point where you can look back and laugh about the things that stressed you out and made you uncomfortable, because your perception will be different. Remember, stress has to do with how you perceive a situation, as a threat or as a normal everyday positive challenge.

Take a moment and read the following Spartan saying and try to understand the metaphorical meaning about how someone can enjoy a hassle-free life. When King Agis II (reigned 427–401 BC) was asked how someone was able to be a free person for all his life, he replied laconically, 'by feeling contempt for death' (Greek term *thanou kataphronon*). So, if an individual has reached a point where he or she is not worried about the possibility of death, then one can assume that this specific individual will not worry about everyday stressful situations at all! Just reflect for a while upon this ancient Greek philosophical approach. Does it merit worrying?

In conclusion, before moving to the core chapters of this book and in order to better comprehend the content, you have to be introduced to the concept of stress, to what stress really is and how it can affect individuals both in a positive and in a negative way. Hence, this is what we are going to analyze in the following chapter.

References

Cartledge, P. (2003). *The Spartans: The World of the Warrior-Heroes of Ancient Greece, From Utopia to Crisis and Collapse*. New York: Overlook Press.

Green, G., Emslie, C., O'Neill, D., Hunt, K., & Walker, S. (2010). Exploring the Ambiguities of Masculinity in Accounts of Emotional Distress in the Military Among Young Ex-Servicemen. *Social Science and Medicine*, 71, 1480–1488.

Jones, J. G., & Moorhouse, A. (2007). *Developing Mental Toughness: Gold Medal Strategies for Transforming Your Business Performance*. Mount Vernon, MO: Spring Hill.

Plutarch, & Talbert, R. J. A. (2005). On Sparta. Rev. ed. New York: Penguin.

Weinberg, R. (2010). *Mental Toughness for Sport, Business and Life*. Bloomington, IN: Author House.

3 Grasping the concept of stress

Now that the philosophy and lifestyle behind ancient Spartans have been introduced and explored, let's focus on a topic that has drawn a lot of attention during the last decades. In this chapter, a historical review of stress is made, from early times until now, introducing the development of the concept.

It does not matter how well aware you are of the topic of stress. You might know a lot concerning stress or not too much. It is perfectly fine, because the main reason why you are reading this book is to try to grasp the concept of stress together. In this chapter we will provide you with a brief history of what stress is, how it has evolved through research and how it affects our everyday lives. One thing is certain. In our modern societies, where everything around us moves in a fast-forward pace, it appears that stress has become an inseparable part of human life. According to Palmer, Cooper and Thomas (2003): 'Stress occurs when pressure exceeds your perceived ability to cope', and our aim is not solely to minimize the experienced stress levels but also to improve imperatively your ability to cope.

The stress concept

In Europe, the first appearance of the term stress was during the 14th century, where it was denoted as a sense of hardship and was derived from the Latin word *stringere*, which means to draw tight (Keil, 2004). In addition, the Greek term *strangalizein*, and its synonym in the English language 'to strangle', have common origins and are related to the exertion of pressure (Chrousos, Loriaux & Gold, 1988).

In the beginning it was used mostly in the field of psychosomatic medicine and physics, but it was in 1946 that Hans Selye first mentioned that the ways through which stress affects and is perceived by an individual are unclear and that further examination is needed to fully understand such a popular concept. While at that time period there was no unique definition of stress, the terms 'stressor' and 'strain' were widely used. 'Stressor' referred to the environmental stimulus that could exert pressure on an individual (i.e. working long hours), and 'strain' referred to the individual response that could be expressed either physically, psychologically or behaviourally.

During the exploration of the stress concept, researchers were mainly focused on three particular approaches:

1   Stress as the dependent variable (the response): stress is viewed as a response to a stimulus that arises from an upsetting situation or the environment, e.g. work overload or harmful environmental settings. Responses may be physiological or behavioural.
2   Stress as the independent variable (the stimulus): stress is viewed as an external phenomenon that acts upon the individual, but without taking into consideration the importance of an individual's perceptions and past experiences. Stress is considered as a disturbing environmental factor.
3   Stress as the intervening variable (the interactionist approach): stress is viewed as the interaction between individuals' perceptions and their responses towards an external stimulus. In other words, stress refers to the lack of fit that exists between the individual and the environment, and it is the combination of both the stimulus and the response approach (Fisher, 1986).

1.   Stress as the dependent variable: response-based definitions

Stress can be tracked historically back to the 18th century, where it was used mostly in the field of science and engineering as a concept to describe the force or pressure that was placed upon a material object or person. In such cases, strain was reflected as the resulting distortion on the object/subject under study (Kahn & Byosiere, 1992).

In 1935 the stress definition was transferred into psychosomatic medicine and biology by Sir Walter Cannon under the 'fight or flight' theory. Cannon's main interest was to investigate the physiological reaction of individuals and animals when they encountered a perceived threat, such as extreme cold or lack of oxygen. Such reactions dictate either a 'fight or flight' mode where the organism either stays and confronts the threat or, if the threat is perceived as overwhelming, flees. The easiest way to picture that is to imagine the reactions of a cat when under the perception of threat. When a cat feels threatened it takes a stiff, straight-legged upright stance. At this precise point it decides whether to fight or take flight, with its back legs heading forward (to fight) and its front legs heading backwards (to flight). A pure physiological response to stress! When it comes to humans, this is the most common reaction to a stressful threat.

Another important topic when we discuss stress refers to the concept of homeostasis in the human organism, a concept that was also introduced by Cannon in 1939. Homeostasis as a principle of equilibrium in everyday life was firstly introduced by ancient Greek philosophers. It was first Empedocles (500–430 BC) around 450 BC who stated that all matter and its elements should coexist in a harmonious balance, followed by Hippocrates (460–375 BC), who linked the theory to human beings relating health to harmonious balance and disease to disharmony (Chrousos, Loriaux & Gold, 1988).

Homeostasis refers to the establishment of an internal balance in every living organism. Homeostasis is not static but generally is considered quite stable over time. Every individual's internal balance is disrupted under the perception of a potential threat. At this point corrective mechanisms, in the form of negative feedback that tries to reverse the original change that was created in a system of the body, come into play, with the aim to restore homeostasis. However, if the threat persists, then corrective mechanisms can prove ineffective, thus causing the manifestation of a disease.

From the response-based approach one can comprehend that a number of seemingly harmless stimuli can act as stressors upon an individual, depending of course on whether the individual perceives them as a threat, something that varies from person to person. A stimulus that can act as a disturbing factor for one person might pass unnoticed for someone else, and vice versa. This depends on personality characteristics, previous life experiences and learning, which are unique factors for every individual. It is clear in this approach that stress acts as an environmental factor that disrupts the individual, and it is viewed from a physiological/medical perspective in an effort to diagnose and treat the signs of stress and not necessarily taking under consideration the causes of stress.

It was not until 1956 that the actual process of stress and its relation to illness was presented by Hans Selye, through the General Adaptation Syndrome (GAS) model. The General Adaptation Syndrome presents the mechanism of stress based on three stages, namely the 'alarm' stage, the 'resistance' stage and the 'exhaustion' stage. The alarm stage is the initial reaction of the organism to deal with stress, both physically and psychologically. As beautifully stated by Selye (1982), it is 'the body's call to arms'; it is the point where the individual enters the stress arena. As presented previously, it can be paralleled with the 'fight or flight' response to an emergency, where the organism activates the sum of its resources to deal with the threat.

We need to understand that this is a never-ending story in our everyday lives, where such a mechanism works numerous times throughout the day, whether we understand it or not, depending on the magnitude of the threat. We also need to be aware that the perceived magnitude and the effects of a stressor can be moderated through experience and through the use of effective coping mechanisms that can improve our wellbeing and calmness levels. These coping mechanisms are going to be elaborated upon later in detail as we unfold the pages of this book.

When the threat is negligible, only the alarm stage reactions are put in place to deal with it, but if the threat is persistent then we pass to the resistance stage, where increased energy consumption is required to deal with the threat and where higher effort is needed to restore an organism's balance. Furthermore, if the threat is prolonged and all defence/coping mechanisms fail to confront and deal with it, the organism is led to the exhaustion stage, where we reach a total depletion of organism's resources – a fact that could even lead to death. Selye (1956) stated that the response of the organism to stress was not related to the environmental stressor itself, but rather it was the individual's perception and response towards the stressor that determined the resulting outcome.

What we need to clarify early in this book is that stress is not necessarily a bad thing! Stress can be distinguished in four components, namely hypostress, eustress, hyperstress and distress (Selye, 1979). Hypostress can be described as a state where there are not many demands for the individual, a condition of understress or a period of boredom. Stress does not exist in this case, but also no excitement or any level of performance can be found here; generally the individual is in a hypotonic phase.

We must learn not to fear stress because stress is not always bad, it is not something alien and it is a process or mechanism that manifests itself within us either physically, psychologically or in both ways. In order to feel alive or perform well in every aspect of our daily life we need portions of stress that will fuel us to make it through the day. This type of healthy stress is called eustress, and every human being has his or her own level of stress tolerance, meaning how much stress he or she can handle before stress becomes disturbing (Cooper & Payne, 1988). In order to understand this concept, let's imagine stress as an inverted U curve. As stress levels increase, we leave the hypostress phase and we enter into the eustress phase, where performance levels also increase in a positive and exciting way.

Eustress extends until it reaches the highest point of the inverted U curve, where the individual reaches his or her maximum level of performance, or reaches the peak. As stated previously, this peak point differs from person to person, indicating that individual differences, past experiences and learning account for the differences in stress tolerance. After this specific peak point, the accumulated pressure and stress levels increase in volume and overwhelm the capability of the individual to manage the demands, and consequently after this point performance starts deteriorating due to the fact that disturbing symptoms enter into the equation, disorienting the individual and leading towards the condition of hyperstress. If hyperstress levels persist and increase, the person collapses and can only perform in minimum levels, thus leading to distress and possibly to the manifestation of disease (both physiological and/or psychological) (Selye, 1979). With that said, our aim in our everyday lives should be to manage and operate within the eustress phase, to learn to observe and regulate our emotions and feelings – in other words to become observers of ourselves and take action to reduce discomfort and distress through the process of self-regulation (Carver & Scheier, 1998). It is okay, though, if sometimes due to an overwhelming day we become distressed; what is important is to be able to accept and understand what is happening to us and utilize all our resources to alleviate stress and smoothly return to the eustress phase again. It is true that in the beginning such a task will not be easy, but be sure that every time you attempt to overcome stress things will gradually become easier.

2. Stress as the independent variable: a stimulus-based approach

This approach views stress as an external factor, suggesting that external stressors are the primary causes for the levels of strain experienced by the individual (Cox, 1978). It was in the 5th century BC when Hippocrates, the Greek physician, asserted that the external environment could affect overall wellbeing and illness.

In other words, stress is perceived as an independent variable, that is, as an external factor that is responsible for the experience of stress that may lead to distress and anxiety. Such a definition of stress is derived as a theory from the physical sciences, and particularly from the science of engineering.

So, on the one hand we have the response-based approach, which is more physiological, and on the other hand we have the stimulus-based approach, which is influenced by the expansion of industrialization, with the aim to create work conditions that will enhance and boost productivity levels. Thus, the focus of stress research shifts on concepts such as temperature, lighting, noise levels etc. (Cox, 1978).

In order to understand this assumption, take into consideration the research made by Sir Raymond Symonds (1947, as cited by Williams, 1947) who examined the cause for the manifested psychological disorders that were disturbing Royal Air Force pilots. Symonds noted, concerning the flying activity, that stress is an external force that is placed upon the individual and not something that is expressed internally; it is the physical forces of the flight, such as speed, altitude and pressure, that create the stress and how the individual perceives the flying process.

It must be noted here that the stimulus-based approach was widely accepted in the work environment because numerous external stressors exist in the work context that are critical and significantly affect employee wellbeing. For this reason, researchers began to investigate the relationship between stress and the office environment in terms of environmental factors such as noise, temperature and pollution (Cooper & Smith, 1985; Vischer, 2005; Vischer, 2007; Misra & Stokols, 2012), as well as the concept of office ergonomics, which covers topics such as the operation of desktop computers, proper desk sitting, illumination and thermal environment (Greenstein & Arnaut, 1987).

Although the stimulus-based approach was met with enthusiasm, it also faced criticism due to the fact that it does not take into consideration individual differences and the fact that a situation or event will be stressful only if the person perceives it as stressful (Lazarus, 1966; Goldberg, 1993). It seems that one of the major limitations of both the stimulus- and response-based models is that they interpret stress as a static phenomenon, whereas in reality stress is a complex phenomenon with a number of variables influencing the resulting impact of stress on an individual. Only the stimulus is not enough to explain the manifestation of stress, because the impact of stimulus can be moderated by personality characteristics, core beliefs, values and learning. This does not take into account the whole process of stress; rather, it views stress only from one dimension. Factors such as the magnitude, duration and severity of the stressor seem to be overlooked, although they are critical for the overall impact and experienced levels of stress. However, the same is evident for the response-based approach, where, although any response can be seen as an outcome of stress, little attention has been given to the duration and severity of them.

Acknowledging the aforementioned criticisms, both for the stimulus and the response approach, the scientific community proposed a third approach to the study of stress, namely the interactionist approach (Cooper, Dewe & O'Driscoll, 2001), an approach that combines:

1   The source/stimulus of the stressful situation,
2   The individual's perception of the situation and
3   The resulting response of the individual.

3.   *An interactionist-based approach*

Based on the interactionist approach, stress is not a static phenomenon; on the contrary, it is a complex process. It is clear today and supported by many researchers for decades now (Cox, 1978; Cooper, Sloan & Williams, 1988) that for an individual to experience disturbing levels of stress, a relationship between the individual and the environment must exist.

Stress has to do with the 'degree of fit' between these two variables. According to person–environment fit theory (P–E; French, Caplan &

Harrison, 1982), a balance between the personality characteristics of an individual (e.g. skills, beliefs, wants) and the characteristics of the environment (e.g. demands) can have a positive effect on an individual's physical and psychological wellbeing, whereas an imbalance between personality characteristics and the environment can create negative feelings and discomfort, thus leading to physical and psychological strain. Such environmental demands can be labelled as either quantitative and/or qualitative in nature, and the individual's skills and beliefs can be considered as the available resources that are utilized in order to cope with the existing demands (French, Caplan & Harrison, 1982).

What can be clearly understood from the interactionist approach is that it is not the environment per se that is stressful, but rather it is the relationship between the person and the environment that may lead to the experience of stress. The interactionist approach has been widely supported and examined by Lazarus (Lazarus, 1966; Lazarus & Launier, 1978, Lazarus & Folkman, 1984; Lazarus, 1993). More specifically, Lazarus and Launier (1978) state that stress can be considered as a situation where the demands placed upon an individual surpass the individual's abilities to overcome them, thus generating feelings of distress.

Lazarus (1966) revealed that stressful conditions did not necessarily resulted in negative effects. Although for certain individuals, the stress levels due to a certain situation had increased immensely, for others the same situation was considered insignificant. How much we are affected by stress depends on the meaning that we ascribe to it in any given situation. According to Lazarus (1993), a stressful appraisal can mean that the situation is viewed as harmful, threatening or challenging:

- Harm refers to a condition where damage has already happened, such as an injury or an illness. A harmful appraisal can generate, among other things, feelings of sadness, anger and disappointment.
- Threat refers to a condition where there is an anticipation of harm which is not evident yet. A threatening appraisal can generate, among other things, feelings of fear, anxiety and worry.
- Challenge refers to a condition where an individual experiences feelings of confidence in overcoming difficult demands utilizing all available coping resources. A challenging appraisal can generate, among other things, feelings of anticipation and/or excitement.

Moreover, Lazarus (1993) noted that each of these views of stressful appraisals can yield diverse consequences. For instance, a threat and the unpleasant feelings that might arise may block mental capacity and diminish performance, whereas challenge through feelings of excitement may boost motivation and significantly increase performance levels.

The whole stress process is determined by how well an individual, taking under consideration an individual's personal attributes, is able to interact with the environment and manage effectively any potential threat. We must understand that stress is not solely an external factor derived from environmental pressure. Stress also depends on an individual's perception or appraisal of the external factor or stimuli, whether or not the stimulus is considered as a threat and to what extent it affects the individual both physically and psychologically.

Hence, the experience of stress is the outcome of a cognitive appraisal, which according to Lazarus (1993) is the process that informs us whether a situation will be perceived as stressful or nonstressful. Such an appraisal relies on a number of factors, i.e. how strong the demand is, previous experiences, personality traits and available resources that an individual possesses in the effort to manage the demanding situation. Furthermore, Lazarus (1993) asserted that cognitive appraisal is divided into primary and secondary appraisal:

- Primary appraisal: The phase where the individual assesses whether the stimulus or stressor has any significance towards an individual's wellbeing and can be characterized either as negative (stressful), neutral or positive.
- Secondary appraisal: The phase after the individual has assessed a situation as demanding and stressful, where consideration is made of available coping resources (i.e. stamina, morale, social support, problemsolving skills) that will be used to manage the disturbing condition.

The central purpose of our book is to blend the science behind stress and resilience, topics that, although extensively studied, still occupy our everyday lives, where we are in a constant search, consciously and subconsciously, to find ways to deal with our daily ups and downs. However, the historical traces of the concepts of stress and resilience go back thousands of years ago to a time where human beings strived for their survival. Of course our modern lives are also demanding and stressful, but in a different way. Today, for instance, we have to deal with technology and mental overload, disturbing factors indeed, but overall there are ways and techniques in place in order to alleviate the negative symptoms of stress.

Times change and we humans have to adjust, but the feelings, emotions and biological reactions of the human organism concerning stress have remained unchanged throughout the centuries.

The biology of stress

Closing this chapter, we will provide you a brief analysis of the biological process of stress, that is, how our bodies are dealing with stress internally, literally through an autonomous process.

As stated in the beginning of the chapter, the existence of the human organism is closely related to the maintenance of an equilibrium, i.e. homeostasis (Cannon, 1939), which is endlessly challenged by stressors of both intrinsic and extrinsic nature. We already analyzed what is happening from a psychological aspect, but how does the process of stress manifest itself from a neuroendocrine, cellular and molecular perspective?

When the stress system is activated with an aim to manage a potential stressor, a number of behavioural and physical changes take place inside the body. If you are interested to know what is happening in the inside, dedicate some time to read the following information; if not, move on to subsequent chapters to learn how to increase your resilience levels and fight against stress.

Biological changes inside the body are instigated during the alarm stage of the General Adaptation Syndrome presented by Selye (1946), with an adapting aim to improve the possibilities of survival for the individual (Chrousos & Gold, 1992).

During the stress process, behavioural adaptation of the body involves the following (adapted from Chrousos & Gold, 1992):

• Increased arousal and alertness
• Increased cognition, vigilance and focused attention
• Suppression of feeding behaviour
• Suppression of reproductive behaviour
• Inhibition of gastric motility; stimulation of colonic motility
• Containment of the stress response

During the stress process, physical adaptation of the body involves the following:

• Oxygen and nutrients directed to the CNS and stressed body site(s)
• Altered cardiovascular tone; increased blood pressure and heart rate
• Increased respiratory rate
• Increased gluconeogenesis and lipolysis
• Detoxification from toxic products
• Inhibition of growth and reproductive systems
• Containment of the stress response
• Containment of the inflammatory/immune response

Let's briefly describe how the biological response to stress works (Palmer & Dryden, 1995): When an individual perceives a situation as threatening and overwhelming, neurons begin to send messages from the cerebral cortex and the limbic system towards the hypothalamus. The anterior part of the hypothalamus creates a sympathetic arousal of the autonomic nervous system (ANS), which is the system responsible for regulating the heart, lungs, stomach and blood vessels. The system is called autonomous because it does not require any conscious effort on our behalf; it is automatic (e.g. just think of the way you breathe; it just happens). The ANS comprises: (a) the sympathetic nervous system (SNS) and (b) the parasympathetic nervous system (PNS).

The PNS sends its messages with the use of a neurotransmitter called acetylcholine and is responsible for the:

- Conservation of energy levels,
- Promotion of relaxation of the body and
- Bodily secretions (e.g. tears, saliva, gastric acids) to assist in the protection of the body and to assist digestion.

The SNS sends its messages with the use of a neurotransmitter called noradrenaline and is responsible for the preparation of the body to act, following the pattern of the 'fight or flight' stress response (Cannon, 1935). This preparation, for instance, involves the following:

- An increase of the heart rate
- An increase of perspiration
- An increase in mental activity
- A decrease in blood clotting time
- A reduction of intestinal movement
- An inhibition of digestive secretions and tears.

In the biological stress response, other crucial parts of the body are involved, namely, the thyroid gland, the pituitary gland and the adrenal gland. The adrenal medulla, which is a part of the adrenal glands (located on top of each kidney) and is connected with the SNS, is responsible for the secretion of adrenaline and noradrenaline (catecholamines) when the SNS is active. Both hormones are responsible for a number of biological activities, such as the increase of the heart rate and blood pressure, where adrenaline prepares the body for flight and noradrenaline prepares the body to fight. Furthermore, the pituitary gland (located close to the hypothalamus in the brain area) is activated during stressful stimuli from the anterior hypothalamus and secretes the adrenocorticotrophic hormone (ACTH), which in turn activates the adrenal cortex. The adrenal cortex is accountable for the formulation of cortisol, which is responsible, among other things, for the increase of arterial blood pressure and the possible reduction of lymphocytes, i.e. white blood cells, which are programmed to counteract the invasion of particles and/or bacteria. Hence, high levels of cortisol, if maintained for long periods, deteriorate the effectiveness of the immune system, making us more susceptible to illness. To conclude, the adrenal cortex also secretes the hormones aldosterone and vasopressin (responsible for the increase of blood pressure, leading to hypertension), oxytocin (responsible for the contraction of the uterus) and a thyroid-stimulating hormone that stimulates the thyroid gland to secrete thyroxin (responsible for the increase of respiration, metabolic rate, blood pressure and intestinal motility that can cause diarrhea).

Finally, if the individual manages to overcome the stressful condition, the PNS gets involved and assists the individual to regain homeostasis, that is, to reach equilibrium again.

It is imperative to understand that this instinctive biological reaction has existed for thousands of years, from the beginning of mankind, in order to protect human beings and assist in their survival when in real physical danger. Fortunately, on the one hand, such dangerous conditions are not that usual in our modern developed societies, but on the other hand this biological reaction does not understand that distinction, and unfortunately it can be triggered by everyday hassles, such as car traffic, an important business meeting, heavy workload, important deadlines and so on. We can give examples forever, in terms of potential daily hassles, because in our modern societies everything happens so fast and the obligations are so many that it is nearly impossible to catch up. But we need to comprehend that our to-do list will never end; it is a never-ending project which we have to manage one way or another. Hence, what would be more effective is to equip ourselves with the necessary tools that will in time enhance our coping mechanisms and increase our resilience levels, thus diminishing the negative impact of stress.

In the next chapter we are going to examine the modern work environment and see how it has evolved during the last decades. What are the most prominent occupational stressors, and what will the future work environment be like?

References

Cannon, W. B. (1935). Stresses and Strain of Homeostasis. *The American Journal of the Medical Sciences*, 189, 1–14.

Cannon, W. B. (1939). *The Wisdom of the Body*. New York: W. W. Norton & Co Inc.

Carver, C. S., & Scheier, M. F. (1998). *On the Self-Regulation of Behavior.* New York: Cambridge University Press.

Chrousos, G. P., & Gold, P. W. (1992). The Concepts of Stress System Disorders: Overview of Behavioral and Physical Homeostasis. *JAMA*, 267, 1244–1252.

Chrousos, G. P., Loriaux, D. L., & Gold, P. W. (1988). Mechanisms of Physical and Emotional Stress. *Advances in Experimental Medicine and Biology*, 245.

Cooper, C. L., Dewe, P. J., & O'Driscoll, M. P. (2001). *Organizational Stress: A Review and Critique of Theory, Research, and Applications.* London: Sage.

Cooper, C. L., & Payne, R. (1988). *Causes, Coping and Consequences of Stress at Work.* Hoboken, NJ: John Wiley and Sons.

Cooper, C. L., Sloan, S. J., & Williams, S. (1988). *Occupational Stress Indicator Management Guide.* Windsor: NFER-Nelson.

Cooper, C. L., & Smith, M. J. (1985). *Job Stress and Blue-Collar Work.* London & New York: John Wiley & Sons.

Cox, T. (1978). *Stress.* London: The Macmillan Press.

Fisher, S. (1986). *Stress and Strategy.* London: Erlbaum Associates.

French, J. R. P., Caplan, R. D., & Harrison, R. V. (1982). *The Mechanisms of Job Stress and Strain.* New York: Wiley.

Goldberg, H. (1993). The Structure of Phenotypic Personality Traits. *American Psychological Association*, 48, 26–34.

Greenstein, J. S., & Arnaut, L. Y. (1987). *Human Factors Aspects of Manual Computer Input Devices.* Handbook of Human Factors. New York: Wiley

Kahn, R. L., & Byosiere, P. (1992). Stress in Organisations. *Handbook of Industrial and Organisational Psychology*, 3, 571–650.

Keil, R. M. K. (2004). Coping and Stress: A Conceptual Analysis. *Journal of Advanced Nursing*, 45, 659–665.

Lazarus, R. S. (1966). *Psychological Stress and the Coping Process.* New York: McGraw-Hill.

Lazarus, R. S. (1993). From Psychological Stress to the Emotions: A History of Changing Outlooks. *Annual Review of Psychology*, 44, 1–21.

Lazarus, R. S., & Folkman, S. (1984). *Stress, Appraisal and Coping.* New York: McGraw-Hill.

Lazarus, R. S., & Launier, R. (1978). *Stress-Related Transactions Between Person and Environment: Perspectives in Interactional Psychology.* New York: Plenum Publishing Corporation.

Misra, S., & Stokols, D. (2012). Psychological and Health Outcomes of Perceived Information Overload. *Environment and Behavior*, 44, 737–759.

Palmer, S., Cooper, C. L., & Thomas, K. (2003). *Creating a Balance: Managing Stress.* London: British Library Board.

Palmer, S., & Dryden, W. (1995). *Counselling for Stress Problems.* London: Sage.

Selye, H. (1946). The General Adaptation Syndrome and the Diseases of Adaptation. *The Journal of Clinical Endocrinology & Metabolism*, 6, 117–230.

Selye, H. (1956). *The Stress of life.* New York: McGraw-Hill.

Selye, H. (1979). Stress, Cancer and the Mind. In J. Tache, H. Selye and S. B. Day (Eds.), *Cancer, Stress and Death* (pp. 1–19). New York: Plenum Medical Book Company.

Selye, H. (1982). History and Present Status of the Stress Concept. In L. Goldberger and S. Breznitz (Eds.), *Handbook of Stress: Theoretical and Clinical Aspects*. New York: Free Press.

Vischer, J. C. (2005). *Space Meets Status: Designing Workplace Performance*. Abingdon: Routledge.

Vischer, J. C. (2007). The Concept of Environmental Comfort in Workplace Performance. *Ambiente Construido, Porto Alegre*, 7, 21–34.

Williams, D. J. (1947). Psychological Problems in Flying Personnel. *British Medical Journal*, 5, 39–42.

4 The modern w@rk terrain

We believe and we are positive that you will agree with us that there was a time, some decades ago, when work, although demanding was more simple, streamlined and linear. This was true for blue-collar and white-collar occupations, both in terms of workload and also in terms of deadlines and pace of work. However, today's employment seems to be closely related to the number 50 for some reason. Fifty years of work until retirement, 50 weeks of work per year and 50 hours of work per week – a work schedule that would appear as something meaningless and weird to our grandparents. A modern work environment is very different, complicated and more demanding when compared to how work used to be some decades ago. This is happening due to a number of factors evident in the workplace that underlie the globalization of the markets and the rapid evolution of technology that have expanded the possibilities for changes in the work context. It is needless to remind to you that all these changes in the work terrain occur in the presence of unstable and insecure societal systems, at such an extent that we have never witnessed before. Many developed countries are facing a pension crisis due to the deep recession and the deterioration of the banking sector, which basically means that employees will be obliged to work for more years until retirement, a fact that will produce detrimental consequences for developed societies as a whole (e.g. higher levels of occupational stress and increased health costs).

To conclude, we have created a 24/7 society that never sleeps in order to satisfy the never-ending human needs for goods, services and our internal urge for constant material consumption. If you think about it, it is a vicious cycle that we have created ourselves when, as a species, we decided to turn our backs on a simpler yet, as many believe, more complete life. The more our needs, the more complicated our lives tend to become. Does this sound familiar to you? Remember that Spartans followed a humble and minimalistic way of life in order to reach excellence and wellbeing. Perhaps it is our turn now to seek and make an effort to exert some control over ourselves and our urges.

Changes in the work terrain

During the last decades, vast changes in the global economy have increased substantially the level of competition not only between companies but also between nations. In addition, in the mid-'90s an increase in stress-related disorders was observed in individuals who worked in schools, hospitals and other public sector entities, due to the fact that competition increased when private companies entered into these industries, thus increasing the level of job insecurity in occupations that until then were considered to be safe. Furthermore, a shift from the manufacturing occupations towards the service occupations created both advantages and disadvantages. On one hand the reduction of manufacturing work had as an effect the occurrence of fewer work accidents and health hazards due to the minimization of manual labour, but on the other hand the service occupations increased rapidly the pace of work globally, affecting negatively both the physical and psychological wellbeing of employees. In the last decades we have witnessed major changes in the work environments in Europe, the US and developed Asian countries that involved fast and intense production requirements, longer hours of work, mergers, downsizing and outsourcing, and a shift from full-time employment to part-time and temporary employment (NIOSH, 2002; Pena-Casas & Pochet, 2009). Nowadays, mental stress has become the most significant health concern, in most occupations, due to the increase of psychosocial demands in the workplace (Pejtersen & Kristensen, 2009). The significance of the potential effects that the modern work environment can have on employees can be demonstrated through the UK government's project on Mental Capital and Wellbeing (Cooper, Field, Goswani, Jenkins & Sahakian, 2009), which examined thoroughly the challenges that the workforce will face during the next decades. Mental capital is defined as:

> The totality of an individual's cognitive and emotional resources, including their cognitive capability, flexibility and efficiency of learning, emotional intelligence and resilience in the face of stress. The extent of an individual's resources reflects his/her basic endowment (genes and early biological programming), and their experiences and education, which take place throughout the lifecourse.
>
> (Cooper, Field, Goswani, Jenkins & Sahakian, 2009)

Mental capital research demonstrated that the work environment will become more challenging and even more complex in the near future and that individuals should and must protect themselves from the negative impact of stress by investing on the development of skills such as resilience and emotional intelligence. Although some initiatives exist from governmental entities and researchers to promote such vital interventions that will assist employees to protect their physical and psychological wellbeing, currently the following question stands: What are you going to do to protect yourself from all the stressors and daily hassles evident in your life? This is the current situation in the work terrain:

- Increased competition
- Increased levels of work pressure and deadlines
- Increased work-life imbalance
- Increased job insecurity
- Increased levels of stress

Now more than ever you have to equip yourself with all the coping mechanisms you can in order to thrive, excel and become the best of your craft, and this is what we are going to elaborate on in the subsequent chapters.

The human element

The improvement of the quality of life in economically developed countries in the European Union, US and Asia has increased life expectancy, thus altering the demographics of the working population. Due to the globalization of the market and the evident job insecurity, more people are forced in a way to work as freelancers or to work under the form of temporary or part-time employment. Employers tend to characterize this as flexible work, but in reality, in the majority of the cases, it is nothing more than part-time work, since organizations are trying to minimize their costs and to achieve their goals with less and more overloaded staff. Such factors have led to the migration of employees from one country to another in a search of a better future.

Such instability gives rise to the manifestation of another phenomenon evident in the work environment, that of negative competition between employees, and thus increases the incidents of bullying at work, a topic that has received attention from the business world during the last decade. For instance, disturbing research findings report that 49.4% from a sample of 5,000 UK employees have been victims or observers of bullying in their workplace within a five-year period (Hoel, Faragher & Cooper, 2004).

The percentage of women who are in search of work or are actively working has increased substantially during the last three decades, varying, however, in terms of percentages from country to country. For instance, although in the US women comprise 51% of the working population, in Italy less than 50% of women are working (The Economist, 2009). Although we are gradually witnessing an increase in the involvement of women in the work environment, according to the World Economic Forum (2015), gender parity is still far away, and urgent interventions should be made to counteract that. In the latest report of the World Economic Forum, its Global Gender Gap Report 2015, it was estimated that it will take 117 years to reach global gender parity in the workplace. It must be noted that in 2014's report the estimation was 81 years, so one can understand the rapid changes that exist in the modern work environment. In addition, concerning the female population, the 'glass ceiling' effect that is defined as an invisible organizational obstacle that restricts access to female workers when it comes to promotion in upper management positions (Davidson & Cooper, 1992) is still evident in our times, although the situation has improved significantly. According to latest data, women held 19.9% of Standard & Poor's 500 board director's seats in 2015 (Catalyst, 2015). Such a percentage seems better when compared with data of earlier reports, which demonstrated that the percentage of female directors in Australia, Canada, the US, South Africa and Europe was estimated to be 8.7%, 12%, 14.7%, 11.5% and 9.7%, respectively (EOWA, 2006; EPWN, 2010). At this point, one should take under consideration what we discussed in the first chapters of this book concerning the freedom and respect that Spartan women were experiencing in ancient Sparta. Comparing to women of other Greek city-states one can argue that the so-called 'glass ceiling' effect did not exist in Sparta. Spartans understood the significance of women in society as a whole. For this reason, we contend that women must be equally respected in the work, family and societal environment. The philosophy and values of the Spartan W@rker do not make distinctions, neither in terms of sex, religion or cultural background. Anyone can become a Spartan W@rker and increase levels of resilience while at the same time decreasing levels of stress. Keep in mind that all the skills that you will learn in the subsequent chapters of this book are not applicable only in your working life. These skills are universal and will help you see and deal with all aspects of life in a more positive and energetic way. You will find pleasure and joy within every activity that you undertake, either at work or at your personal life. Who wouldn't want that?

To continue, in terms of the modern workforce, we are witnessing an increasing shift in dual-career women and also two-earner families, which on the one hand seems beneficial in terms of higher family income but on the other hand seems to be a main cause of conflict in the family roles and work–life balance. Demanding work schedules, when paired with a number of obligations that need to be addressed in employees' personal lives, lead to the depletion of employees' resources, exhaustion and the experience of disturbing levels of stress. Such factors seem to have been recognized both by high-end companies and governmental bodies that attempt to introduce the concept of flexible work arrangements, since flexibility at work has been found to diminish work–life conflict and also to promote the psychological wellbeing of workers (O'Driscoll, Poelmans, Spector, Kalliath, Allen, Cooper & Sanchez, 2003).

Technology

Specialists in the early 1970s proclaimed that we have reached the age of technology, which would be responsible for the advancement of the work environment and would make the life of employees and the business world stress free, reaching a 20-hour workweek and an ideal and most importantly healthy way of living. Well, although we find technology very helpful in the work domain, unfortunately, it did not work that way.

The way through which technology has altered the meaning and the significance of work as we knew it is remarkable. During the last decades, the use of mobile devices (i.e. phones, tablets and laptops) in conjunction with email and the expansion of the Internet has transformed the work environment and the pace of work completely. The exchange of information is continuous, and information can access you wherever you may be, thus increasing the workload and creating a mismatch between work and life balance.

The vast expansion of the use of information technology has led to an increase of work pace and to information overload, which has a negative impact on employees' health (Jackson & Cooper, 1997). Although theory suggests that employees benefit from the receipt of information at work, since it helps them to perform their duties more effectively, there is a point where individuals reach their biological limits and are unable to handle any additional incoming information, thus becoming overwhelmed and stressed (Eppler & Mengis, 2004; Misra & Stokols, 2012). When an individual is overloaded from information, then the ability to perform adequately is reduced, overall performance deteriorates substantially and feelings of confusion and incapability helplessness tend to emerge (Jacoby, 1977; Schick, Gorden & Haka, 1990; Eppler & Mengis, 2004). Such an increasing reliance on information technology has increased substantially what experts report as 'screen time', and a plethora of studies have supported that prolonged periods of time dedicated in front of visual display terminals (VDTs) can negatively affect employees' health, both physically (i.e. musculoskeletal injuries, visual problems, headaches) and psychologically (i.e. psychological stress, irritation and fatigue) (Ekberg, Eklund, Tuvesson, Oertengren, Odenrick & Ericson, 1995; Aaras, Horgen & Ro, 2000; Misra & Stokols, 2012).

If you consider this for a while, it seems inevitable and requires very good individual skills that will help you to organize your time appropriately and to protect your personal life from technology and information overload.

In the past, even when email and the Internet were present, you could sustain your work–life balance due to the fact that mobile technology was still absent. Even if you had a significant amount of emails and tasks to perform during your office work schedule, when you left the office, you were also leaving your 'to-do' list at work. The only think you had to do before you went on to continue your day was to schedule your work priorities and tasks for the next day. After that you were practically unreachable, because without the extended use of mobile phones, mobile emails, SMS, notifications and social media, nobody could have access to you, unless it was a serious emergency. But today, technology seems to have become addictive in a way, and we feel that we must always be connected in some way or else we might feel isolated and unimportant within an organization. For example, some individuals might feel frustrated or sad if they come to hear that the previous night there was a business emergency and that a number of colleagues were called to act upon the emergency but no one has informed them. Furthermore, the feelings of stress and the insecurity due to the turbulent economic times that we are witnessing also are increasing due to technology and the use of electronic performance monitoring of the time that employees spent on their computers and their communication (Carayon, 1994).

Fostering general wellbeing

As mentioned previously, the continuous transformation of the work environment in the last decades along with the rapid societal changes create an unstable work context and increase employees' feelings of insecurity.

We are observers of radical changes in organizational structures and managerial styles due to the fact that the organizations seek to remain competitive in the market and manage their progress and survival through the global economic crisis. By doing so, though, organizations jeopardize and put at risk the social, ethical and HR elements of the work context, aiming only to achieve financial growth no matter the cost. This reality demanded and turned the focus of interest on research with the aim to explain the new face of organizational life and to pay attention not to the economic element but rather to the social element of organizational life (Ghoshal, 2005). Now more than ever emerges the need to assess and promote the positive elements of the work environment. We need to promote a sense of wellbeing that will eventually lead to feelings of happiness within the workforce, even during turbulent and demanding times. But, please do not be confused: happiness does not only require a high-status well paid job, but it rather is the end result of a sense of job control, feeling valued and trusted, the existence of good work relationships and of course the flexibility that will enable you to preserve a rewarding and healthy work–life balance (Lundberg & Cooper,

2010). To earn this, though, you must become a necessary and fundamental part of your work environment; you must become a Spartan W@rker who can manage every difficult situation – a Spartan W@rker who, even when unable to manage a situation alone, can succeed through the beneficial work social support network that he/she has created by demonstrating extraordinary interpersonal, communication and teamwork skills. You must lead by example, and when it comes to leadership, you do not have to have a title to lead: you can lead within a team by providing support and valuable input towards organizational success. There is only one person whom you have to lead and manage to succeed in this demanding work terrain, and that is no one but yourself. It is what you do in your everyday life and how you develop yourself in concepts such as resilience, mental toughness and emotional intelligence that will dictate the person you will become in the near future. It does not matter where you stand now; it is never too late to embrace the philosophy of the Spartan W@rker, where you never give up because, as we maintain: 'If you never give up then you cannot fail.' If you keep on enriching and advancing yourself in all the concepts that we present you throughout this book, you will continually evolve to a better self with more skills and resources to manage your life. After all, this is what everyone wants: a stress-free manageable life, where even when adversities appear we embrace them with a positive view and attitude.

Summary

In this chapter, the current situation evident in the modern work environment was presented with an aim to see where we stand now and what we need to consider in order to manage our everyday lives, succeed at work and protect our wellbeing. In the next chapter we go deeper and explore the concept of occupational stress by presenting the cost of stress at work, the most influential work-stress models and the most critical occupational sources of stress that we must deal with.

References

Aaras, A., Horgen, G., & Ro, O. (2000). Work With the Visual Display Unit: Health Consequences. *International Journal of Human-Computer Interaction*, 12, 107–134.

Carayon, P. (1994). Effects of Electronic Performance Monitoring on Job Design and Worker Stress: Results of Two Studies. *International Journal of Human-Computer Interaction*, 6, 177–190.

Catalyst (2015). *Catalyst Census: Women and Men Board Directors*. New York: Catalyst, 2016.

Cooper, C. L., Field, J., Goswani, U., Jenkins, R., & Sahakian, B. (Eds.). (2009). *Mental Capital and Wellbeing*. Oxford: Wiley-Blackwell.

Davidson, M. J., & Cooper, C. L. (1992). *Shattering the Glass Ceiling: The Woman Manager*. London: Paul Chapman.

Economist, The (2009). *Female Power*. 30 December.

Ekberg, K., Eklund, J., Tuvesson, M., Oertengren, R., Odenrick, P., & Ericson, M. (1995). Psychological Stress and Muscle Activity During Data Entry at Visual Display Units. *Work and Stress*, 9, 475–490.

Eppler, M. J., & Mengis, J. (2004). The Concept of Information Overload: A Review of Literature From Organization Science, Accounting, Marketing, MIS, and Related Disciplines. *The Information Society*, 20, 325–344.

Equal Opportunity for Women in the Workplace Agency (EOWA). (2006). *Australian Census of Women in Leadership 2006*. www.wgea.gov.au/sites/default/files/2006_EOWA_Census_Publication_tagged.pdf

European Professional Women's Network (EPWN). (2010). *Fourth Bi-Annual European PWN Board Women Monitor 2010*. In Partnership with Russell Reynolds Associates.

Ghoshal, S. (2005) *Bad management theories are destroying good management practices*. Academy of Management Learning and Education 4, 75–91.

Hoel, H., Faragher, B., & Cooper, C. L. (2004). Bullying Is Detrimental to Health, But All Bullying Behaviours Are Not Necessarily Equally Damaging. *British Journal of Guidance and Counselling*, 32, 367–387.

Jackson, S. E., & Cooper, C. L. (Eds.). (1997). *Creating Tomorrow's Organizations: A Handbook for Future Research in Organizational Behavior*. New York: Wiley.

Jacoby, J. (1977). Information Load and Decision Quality: Some Contested Issues. *Journal of Marketing Research*, 14, 569–573.

Lundberg, U. & Cooper, C. L. (2010) *The Science of Occupational Health: Stress, Psychobiology and the New World of Work*. Oxford: Wiley-Blackwell.

Misra, S., & Stokols, D. (2012). Psychological and Health Outcomes of Perceived Information Overload. *Environment and Behavior*, 44, 737–759.

Niosh, N. (2002). *The Changing Organization of Work and the Safety and Health of Working People*. Technical Report 2002–116. National Institute for Occupational Safety and Health (NIOSH).

O'Driscoll, M. P., Poelmans, S., Spector, P. E., Kalliath, T., Allen, T. D., Cooper, C. L., & Sanchez, J. I. (2003). Family-Responsive Interventions, Perceived Organizational and Supervisor Support, Work – Family Conflict, and Psychological Strain. *International Journal of Stress Management*, 10, 326–344.

Pejtersen, J. H., & Kristensen, T. S. (2009). The Development of the Psychosocial Work Environment in Denmark From 1997 to 2005. *Scandinavian Journal of Work, Environment & Health*, 35, 284–293.

Pena-Casas, R., & Pochet, P. (2009). *Convergence and Divergence of Working Conditions in Europe: 1990–2005*. European Foundation for the Improvement of Living and Working Conditions, Dublin.

Schick, A. G., Gorden, L. A., & Haka, S. (1990). Information Overload: A Temporal Approach. *Accounting, Organizations and Society*, 15, 199–220.

World Economic Forum. (2014). *Global Gender Gap Report*. http://reports.weforum.org/global-gender-gap-report-2014/

World Economic Forum. (2015). *Global Gender Gap Report*. http://reports.weforum.org/global-gender-gap-report-2015/

5 The occupational stress arena

We spend approximately one-third of our adult life in our work environment – the best and more energetic years of our lives. Basically, if we consider that an average human being sleeps around eight hours per day, and we exclude weekends, we spend around 50% of our free time at work. If we consider the fact that the majority of the occupations up to now exceed the eight hours of work per day, adding also the time spent going back and forth to reach our workplace, along with the time consumed for the emails and the mobile technology that follows us everywhere, then one can really wonder how much free and quality time do we have in our disposition in order to spend for ourselves and with our loved ones in our everyday lives. Was that sentence too long for you to read? Well, metaphorically this is how long your work day most probably is . . . Through these statements, a philosophical question arises:

Are you working to live, or are you living to work?

Did this assumption made you think your own reality? Are we somehow describing here your lifestyle? Do you feel stressed even by thinking of it? Well, simply put, these are all small signs of occupational stress, the result of when stress interferes and distorts our personal lives, leading to work–life imbalance. But what exactly is occupational stress, and why should we be bothered to read about it? To put you on track and catch your attention, let's start this chapter by providing you with a brief analysis of the costs of stress at work, both in terms of health and financial costs.

Cost of occupational stress

Let's start by stating epigrammatically a number of physical and psychological symptoms of stress that an individual can experience during difficult and demanding periods at work based on A Short Stress Evaluation Tool (ASSET; Faragher, Cooper & Cartwright, 2004). ASSET is a well-established questionnaire examining occupational stress upon which we are going to base our discussions throughout this book concerning the concept of stress and the development of resilience. The ASSET model measures the levels of stress in any working environment, taking into consideration the most critical occupational stressors. Moreover, ASSET provides information on employees' current state of physical health, psychological wellbeing, organizational commitment and self-rated productivity.

The effect of stress on employees' physical health

- Lack of appetite or overeating
- Indigestion or heartburn
- Insomnia – sleep loss
- Headaches
- Muscular tension/aches and pains
- Feeling nauseous or being sick

The effect of stress on employees' mental health

- Panic or anxiety attacks
- Constant irritability
- Difficulty in making decisions
- Loss of sense of humour
- Feeling or becoming angry with others too easily
- Constant tiredness
- Feeling unable to cope
- Avoiding contact with other people
- Mood swings
- Unable to listen to other people
- Having difficulty concentrating

Experiencing one or more of these negative symptoms does not mean that our wellbeing is in danger. Other variables may be accountable for these symptoms, and also the duration of the stress threat may be of a short-term nature. The problem arises when such symptoms are frequent and present for a prolonged period of time and when we are choosing to neglect them rather than giving them the necessary attention, thus jeopardizing our wellbeing and the wellbeing of our loved ones.

Not being able to address the topic of occupational stress and find ways to counteract its negative consequences can have significant costs for both the individual and the organization as well. Although the financial costs of the business industry will be presented, of paramount importance are the individual costs that employees experience during everyday work interactions and also the individual costs that employees experience in their personal life through the form of the spill-over effect. The spill-over effect suggests that the stress experienced at work can be transferred into employees' personal lives with undesirable consequences for employees' physical and psychological wellbeing (O'Driscoll, 1996). It seems that we have reached the point where we need to check within every form of work environment and find ways both at an individual and organizational level to control the stress levels experienced by employees, thus protecting workers' overall health along with their levels of job satisfaction and productivity (Cartwright & Cooper, 2009).

For this reason, we believe that managing stress at a personal level is the best route to preserve physical and psychological wellbeing, by seriously training yourself to the accumulation of skills that will assist you towards this venture. On another note, the same stands also for organizations that embrace a wellbeing culture and mentality towards their staff. It does not matter if you are an employee, an owner of a large corporation or an owner of a small local store. Through appreciating and being committed towards the wellbeing of your colleagues, you invest indirectly in your own wellbeing, due to the fact that you will be surrounded by positive, happy and most importantly nontoxic people who embrace the Spartan W@rker philosophy.

To begin with, a few years ago the Centre for Mental Health (2007) released an alarming report which said that the cost of stress and mental illness in the UK has reached the amount of 26 billion UK pounds annually for cases of labour turnover, absenteeism and presenteeism (interestingly, presenteeism costs were two times increased the costs of absenteeism). Moreover, the financial cost concerning individuals who are unable to work due to illness reached the amount of 12 billion UK pounds annually, with stress and mental illness being responsible for 40% of the amount. From this data one can understand that workers are experiencing a number of health concerns due to stress, something also supported by the Health and Safety Executive (HSE) report in 2007, which stated that approximately 500,000 employees were disturbed due to heightened levels of occupational stress, negatively affecting their wellbeing (Cartwright & Cooper, 2009). Similarly, the International Survey Program (ISP), a survey that involved 15 OECD countries, indicated that employees who experienced symptoms of occupational stress reached 80% (Clarke & Cooper, 2004). This seems disturbing, especially when the evaluated long-term consequences of stress can pose a serious health threat and considering that in 2005, 63,000 employees supported that they were patients of heart disease caused by work factors and by the experience of chronic stress (Cooper, Field, Goswani, Jenkins & Sahakian, 2009). Negative findings have also been reported from earlier studies, which demonstrate the fact that the condition has not improved through the years. For instance, the British Heart Foundation Coronary

Prevention Group reported that 180,000 people die annually due to coronary heart disease, a statistic that has been associated with chronic stress (Cartwright & Cooper, 1997). Similarly, concerning the relationships between stress and illness, stress has been linked with stroke, cancer, thyroid gland malfunctions, asthma, arthritis, migraines, high blood pressure and ulcers (Cooper, Cooper & Eaker, 1988; Greenberg, 2009). Furthermore, reports published by the Health and Safety Executive (HSE, 2001) support that acute and chronic stress are related to numerous health complaints such as gastrointestinal problems, cardiovascular diseases and depression, as well as to several unhealthy habits such as smoking, alcohol consumption, drug use and obesity, which in turn, can precipitate the manifestation of ill health.

Going back to the cost of absenteeism and labour turnover, in 2007 the Confederation of British Industry reported that the direct cost of absenteeism in the UK is calculated as 537 UK pounds per employee annually, with a supplementary indirect cost per employee of 270 UK pounds. In total, the Confederation of British Industry estimated that the cost of absenteeism per annum is higher than 10 billion pounds (Palmer & Cooper, 2007). In addition, the UK's Health and Safety Executive assessed that 60% of work absences are related to sickness due to stress and calculated that 40 million working days are lost due to absenteeism annually (Earnshaw & Cooper, 2001).

Employees who are unable to go to work due to stress symptoms is a common phenomenon nowadays, and its negative costs, both financial and in terms of employees' health, are tangible and easier to measure. What is considered more difficult to evaluate and gauge, though, is the cost of presenteeism, where although employees are present at work, they are unable to perform adequately due to experienced stress or to any other health symptom (Hemp, 2004). This has a double cost, because in case of an absence someone else will probably do the work, but when an employee is present and under stress, it jeopardizes his/her health, and in addition the work is not being done. In a similar report of the Chartered Institute of Personnel and Development (CIPD, 2007) and in terms of labour turnover, it was indicated that the cost of an employee's replacement is approximately 8,000 UK pounds (including the cost of the new recruitment and induction training along with the cost of the lost investment concerning the employee who is leaving).

From all the aforementioned reports, one can understand the severity of the situation when it comes to occupational stress. This is true, especially in light of the Health and Safety Executive stating in 2000 that 20% of the entire working population is suffering from negative symptoms of stress, with the statistics rising to 40% in certain high-risk occupations (Collins & Gibbs, 2003).

It has been supported by the scientific literature that employees with good health are more productive and effective, are absent less often and demonstrate better coping skills against stress (Dupre & Day, 2007; Merrill, Aldana, Pope, Anderson, Coberley, Grossmeier & Whitmer, 2013). Hence, how can an individual reach an optimal level of physical and psychological health? What are the characteristics that differentiate people who are able to deal with everyday hassles from those who seem to be negatively affected by the harsh conditions of the modern work environment and the modern lifestyle? Is this something innate and predetermined or something learned from experience and the development of specific skills? The truth is that certain characteristics become stable features of our personality after a particular age, but there are a plethora of skills and traits that can be learned and developed to such an extent that they can make your life and how you experience things change entirely in a positive and healthy way. Equipping yourself with such assets will transform you both physically and psychologically, make you feel more complete and satisfied in everyday life, and enable you to distinguish and give attention only to the significant things in life, whereas unimportant hassles that once occupied your brain will now just pass in front of your eyes like a cloud, without influencing you at all. Doesn't this scenario seem ideal? Maybe too good to be true? Well, it is true, and it is up to you to control yourself, your emotions, your behaviour and your actions and become what we define as a Spartan W@rker.

Before we start elaborating on the ways through which you can become a Spartan W@rker, we find it important to present to you the scientific theory so far when it comes to influential occupational stress models, which explain how an individual interacts with the work environment, what the most significant stressors evident in the modern work environment are and how all these variables can interplay and negatively affect the employee. More specifically, with this presentation we aim to portray the ways through which occupational stressors may affect several occupational outcomes and employees' overall wellbeing. With this illustration in mind, we can then move on to start the discussion of how we can deal and cope effectively with these occupational stressors.

Models of occupational stress

In our times, as also stated in the beginning of this chapter, the majority of the population devotes approximately half of their waking life at work, and for this reason, the need to examine the impact of occupational stressors on the physical and psychological wellbeing of employees is mandatory. Consequently, many researchers have showed interest in investigating occupational stress, and so in the following pages we present to you some of the most influential models in order to understand how things have evolved over time and where we stand today.

It was early in 1978 that Cox presented the so-called Five Stage Transactional Model, which denoted that stress is the reflecting outcome of individuals' perceptions. Although the model is related to both the stimulus- and response-based models of stress (as analyzed in Chapter 3), it focuses on the transactional nature of the stress phenomena, indicating that stress is a mentally stimulating process that involves both the person and the surrounding environment. More analytically:

- The first stage of the stress equation reflects the demands (internal and external) that are placed upon the individual.
- The second stage involves the individual's perception of the specific demands, as to whether they are stressful or not, and if the individual possesses the ability to cope with them. Stress can be considered as an imbalance between the demand (stressor) and the perception of this demand, a view that comes in accordance with previous stress theories (Lazarus & Folkman, 1984; French, Caplan & Harrison, 1982).
- During the third stage the individual assesses all the existing coping strategies that could be utilized in order to deal with stress, and the third stage also involves the selection of the most suitable one.
- The fourth stage refers to the effect of the preferred coping strategy on the stress equation, assessing whether or not it was successful in dealing with the demand.
- The fifth stage is the general feedback element that is constant and present within all stages of the model, enabling changes to be made to the actions of the individual and to develop new strategies that can be used in future demanding events as a form of coping.

According to Cox, work stress involves both the physical and psychological aspects of the job, and coping satisfactorily with the demands of the job is a complex task that requires effort and substantial allocation of resources from the employees.

One thing is certain for us: In order to deal with stress effectively, you need a well-established course of action that it is in accordance with your own needs and abilities.

Moving on, we need to give credit to Karasek's Job Demand-Control model (JDC; Karasek, 1979), a model that has been used extensively in stress research. The JDC model suggests that the combination of highly demanding jobs that involve long working hours with increased workload, within work environments that allow low levels of job control, increases the stress levels within an organization. In Karasek's model it is asserted that even when high demands are existent within a work environment, the presence of satisfactory levels of job control and autonomy can moderate the negative impact of the work stressors, because being able to take decisions and organize a course of action based on your own view of things and capabilities can reduce stress levels significantly and thus shield your wellbeing.

Although the JDC model has been used successfully in a plethora of research, it has been argued that job control cannot be the only factor to take under consideration when dealing with stress, since stress is considered a complex and multifaceted phenomenon. For this reason, an extension of Karasek's model was proposed, namely the Job Demands-Control-Support (JDCS) model, in which, along with job control work, social support is also taken under consideration as an available resource to deal with the demands of the job and the stress that comes along (Johnson & Hall, 1988). Taking into consideration the buffering hypothesis of the JDCS model, work social support can alleviate the pressure that can be created due to stress in work environments that are characterized by high job demands and low levels of job control.

Nevertheless, limitations still existed in the revised JDCS model, based on the understanding that it is very difficult to map all the stress variables within just three concepts (i.e. job demands, job control and work social support), and in order to overcome them a new model, namely the Job Demand Resources (JDR) model, was presented (Demerouti, Bakker, Nachreiner & Schaufeli, 2001). This model defined job demands as the physical, social or psychological components of work that require both physical and psychological effort from employees. When job demands are intense and prolonged, they can lead to physical and/or mental strain. Moreover, job resources are defined as the physical, social or psychological components of work that assist employees to manage more effectively the demands of the job and also preserve and shield their overall wellbeing (Demerouti, Bakker, Nachreiner & Schaufeli, 2001). An example of job resources at an organizational level could be the availability of proper equipment in the workplace that would help to do the job more effectively, whereas at an individual level those resources could be the existence of positive work relationships with colleagues, promoting a buffering effect in overcoming everyday work demands.

The JDR model involves two processes, namely the strain and the motivational process. The strain process suggests that high and overwhelming job demands require the use of an increased number of physical and psychological resources, thus depleting the energy reserves of the employee, creating distress and threatening his or her wellbeing. On the other hand, the motivational process views available resources in the form of stimulants that facilitate the work process and lead to positive outcomes, such as enhanced performance and work engagement with mutual benefits for both the employee and the organization.

Since we mentioned earlier the concept of job resources and their scarce availability, we need to elaborate a little further on Hobfoll's Conservation of Resources model (COR, 1989). According to Hobfoll, employees are in an endless process of acquiring and preserving resources that will help them perform their work duties more effectively and simultaneously reduce stress levels at work when dealing with demanding conditions. Stress at work can be manifested in three ways:

1 Threat of resource loss
2 Actual resource loss
3 Insufficient attainment of resources.

Since resources are scarce, even the threat of resource loss, meaning reaching a point where the individual perceives that the majority of available resources is depleted (even when this is not the case), increases the experienced levels of stress, thus hindering performance. The situation becomes even harsher when there are no incoming resources (i.e. in the form of work social support) to assist in the difficult condition. Finally, the individual, if the stressful situation is prolonged, reaches a point where all available resources are lost, increasing the negative impact of stress on the employee's wellbeing.

Resources are separated in the following four categories:

• Personal characteristics (e.g. self-esteem, self-efficacy, skills)
• Objects (e.g. material resources such as laptops, printers, adequate Internet connection)
• Conditions (e.g. means that facilitate the process of goal accomplishment)
• Energies (e.g. time, money).

It seems that employees are constantly investing in resources in order to avoid any resource loss and recover fast from any potential resource loss, resulting in an endless quest to increase their reserves of resources. By aiming to increase the reserves of resources, individuals understand the need to continuously expand skills, experience and knowledge based on learning through everyday situations. Overall, such an investment increases the resilience levels, making an individual able to confront any difficult situation at work with the minimum cost of resources loss. The ability to conserve resources better than someone else when dealing with the same situation shows that the resilient individual will remain unaffected and in balance from certain work stressors when compared to a less resilient person, as if the situation was too simple to even constitute a problem in the first place. That is the point where we all want to reach. Think about it: isn't this the ideal scenario?

All this requires certain investment from yourself in order to manage, obtain, maintain, protect and then continuously expand your resources.

What we can understand from these models is that in the stress literature, a never-ending dialogue exists in terms of how stress is defined, how it is measured and what the most critical work stressors are that, if dealt with sufficiently, would lead to a more complete understanding of the concept and to the application of better interventions against stress. Based on the models, researchers understood that the stress phenomenon is quite complex and must be seen from many different angles, including many variables in the equation, in order to be more fully addressed. However, this seems to be an ongoing process, since the modern work environment changes so rapidly. For instance, nowadays we have to deal with certain work stressors that did not exist in the literature two decades ago.

Moving forward, the Occupational Stress Indicator (OSI; Cooper, Sloan & Williams, 1988) was an initial attempt, in the form of a self-reported measure, that aimed to examine the most critical occupational stressors and how they could affect employees' wellbeing. OSI comprised three sections in accordance with the interactionist based approach to stress (i.e. the interaction between the stimulus and the response; see Chapter 3).

The first section presented the most prominent occupational sources of stress:

1 Factors intrinsic to the job
2 Role in the organization
3 Relationships at work
4 Career and achievement
5 Organizational structure and climate
6 Home-work interface.

The second section of the OSI model focused on the importance of three personality characteristics:

1 Type A behaviour
2 Coping strategies
3 Locus of control.

The third section of the OSI demonstrated the effect that the occupational sources of stress have upon:

1 Physical health
2 Mental health
3 Job satisfaction.

Although OSI has been used substantially in workplace stress research during the '90s (from 1990 to 1997, approximately 38 scientific publications exist that used OSI) with the objective to develop more effective stress management techniques and improve wellbeing within the work environment (Evers, Frese & Cooper, 2000), it has not escaped criticism due to its length (160 items) and the inclusion of some personality characteristics that were not found to report satisfactory reliability coefficients in a number of studies (Lyne, Barrett, Williams & Coaley, 2000). An improved version of OSI, namely Pressure Management Indicator (PMI; Williams & Cooper, 1998), which was shorter (120 items) and included some new elements such as was the concept of resilience, was presented to address these limitations. However, some limitations were still evident, and based on the fact that the work environment had changed significantly within the 15 years since the development of OSI, Cartwright and Cooper (2002) designed A Short Stress Evaluation Tool (ASSET) (Figure 5.1). The benefit of ASSET is that, when compared to other occupational stress models, it views work stressors in a combination rather than separately, and it also calculates their cumulative effect on employee's wellbeing. ASSET, like its ancestor OSI, is also divided into three sections.

The first section includes the following work stressors scales:

1   Work relationships
2   Work-life balance
3   Overload
4   Job security
5   Control
6   Resources and communication
7   Pay and benefits
8   Aspects of the job.

The second section of ASSET concerns levels of commitment, incorporating two types:

1   Commitment of the organization to the employee
2   Commitment of the employee to the organization.

Finally, the third section examines employees':

1   Physical health
2   Psychological wellbeing
3   Self-rated productivity.

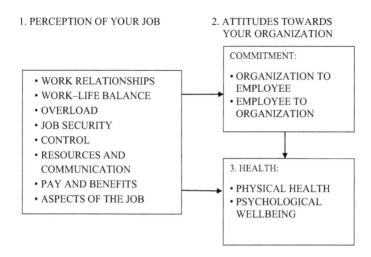

Figure 5.1 ASSET model

Source: Faragher, Cooper & Cartwright (2004).

The ASSET model is applicable in all occupational settings (both blue collar and white collar occupations), and a number of studies provide supporting evidence towards its psychometric properties (Faragher, Cooper & Cartwright, 2004; Donald, Taylor, Johnson, Cooper, Cartwright & Robertson, 2005).

Summary

In this chapter we introduced you briefly to the costs of stress, both in terms of an individual's health and also in terms of financial costs for the organizations and the nations. One thing is certain, interventions must be made in order to protect employees' wellbeing; but rather than just waiting to be saved by someone else, we need to invest in our own strengths and to discover new and alternative ways that will make us resilient to stress. The following chapters will provide you with game-changing techniques that, if practised well, will transform you to something new – will transform you to a Spartan W@rker, to an individual who enjoys work immensely, finds pleasure through constructive challenges and returns back home feeling complete, proud, satisfied and calm, ready to enjoy his/her personal time. We also presented some influential occupational stress models to get a grasp on the scientific approach on stress, and we concluded with the presentation of OSI and ASSET models. The reason why we analyzed the ASSET model thoroughly is that the following chapters, which will explore the ways through which one can become a Spartan W@rker and the Spartan W@ rker's coping techniques, are going to be closely related to how the afore-mentioned occupational stressors of ASSET can have a positive indicator (i.e. feelings of job security rather than depressing feelings of job insecurity), thus keeping the stress equation positive in a eustress stage, which in turns will lead to positive physical health, psychological wellbeing and enhanced levels of productivity. We are going to explore all these techniques both in an individual and environmental level that will promote your wellbeing at work and will help you lead a healthier and more fulfilling personal life.

References

Cartwright, S., & Cooper, C. L. (1997). *Managing Workplace Stress*. London: Sage Publications.

Cartwright, S., & Cooper, C. L. (2002). *ASSET: An Organisational Stress Screening Tool, the Management Guide*. Manchester: RCL Ltd.

Cartwright, S., & Cooper, C. L. (2009). *The Oxford Handbook of Organisational Wellbeing*. Oxford: Oxford University Press.

Chartered Institute of Personnel and Development. (2007). *A Barometer of HR Trends and Prospects 2007: Overview of CIPD Surveys*. London: CIPD Chartered Institute of Personnel and Development.

Clarke, S., & Cooper, C. L. (2004). *Managing the Risk of Workplace Stress*. London: Taylor and Francis Group.

Collins, P. A., & Gibbs, A. C. C. (2003). Stress in Police Officers: A Study of the Origins, Prevalence and Severity of Stress-Related Symptoms Within a County Police Force. *Occupational Medicine*, 53, 256–264.

Confederation of British Industry. (2007). *Employment Trends Survey 2007: Fit for Business*. London: Author.

Cooper, C. L., Cooper, R. D., & Eaker, L. H. (1988). *Living With Stress*. London: Penguin Books Ltd.

Cooper, C. L., Field, J., Goswani, U., Jenkins, R., & Sahakian, B. (Eds.). (2009). *Mental Capital and Wellbeing*. Oxford: Wiley-Blackwell.

Cooper, C. L., Sloan, S. J., & Williams, S. (1988). *Occupational Stress Indicator Management Guide*. Windsor: NFER-Nelson.

Cox, T. (1978). *Stress*. London: The Macmillan Press.

Demerouti, E., Bakker, A. B., Nachreiner, F., & Schaufeli, W. B. (2001). The Job Demands-Resources Model of Burnout. *Journal of Applied Psychology*, 86, 499–512.

Donald, I., Taylor, P., Johnson, S., Cooper, C. L., Cartwright, S., & Robertson, S. (2005). Work Environments, Stress, and Productivity: An Examination Using ASSET. *International Journal of Stress Management*, 12, 409–423.

Dupre, K. E., & Day, A. L. (2007). The Effects of Supportive Management and Job Quality on the Turnover Intentions and Health of Military Personnel. *Human Resource Management*, 46, 185–201.

Earnshaw, J., & Cooper, C. L. (2001). *Stress and Employer Liability*. London: Institute of Personnel and Development (IPD).

Evers, A., Frese, M., & Cooper, C. L. (2000). Revisions and Further Developments of the Occupational Stress Indicator: LISREL Results From Four Dutch Studies. *Journal of Occupational and Organizational Psychology*, 73, 221–240.

Faragher, E. B., Cooper, C. L., & Cartwright, S. (2004). A Shortened Stress Evaluation Tool (ASSET). *Stress and Health*, 20, 189–201.

French, J. R. P., Caplan, R. D., & Harrison, R. V. (1982). *The Mechanisms of Job Stress and Strain*. New York: Wiley.

Greenberg, J. S. (2009). *Comprehensive Stress Management*. New York: McGraw-Hill Companies.

Health and Safety Executive. (2001). *Tackling Work Related Stress*. London: HSE Books.

Hemp, P. (2004, October). Presenteeism: At Work-But Out of It. *Harvard Business Review*, 49–58.

Hobfoll, S. E. (1989). Conservation of Resources: A New Attempt at Conceptualizing Stress. *American Psychologist*, 44, 513–524.

Johnson, J. V., & Hall, E. M. (1988). Job Strain, Workplace Social Support, and Cardiovascular Disease: A Cross-Sectional Study of a Random Sample of the Swedish Working Population. *American Journal of Public Health*, 78, 1336–1342.

Karasek, R. A. (1979). Job Demands, Job Decision Latitude, and Mental Strain: Implications for Job Redesign. *Administrative Science Quarterly*, 24, 285–308.

Lazarus, R. S., & Folkman, S. (1984). *Stress, Appraisal and Coping*. New York: McGraw-Hill.

Lyne, K. D., Barrett, P. T., Williams, C., & Coaley, K. (2000). A Psychometric Evaluation of the Occupational Stress Indicator. *Journal of Occupational and Organizational Psychology*, 73, 195–220.

Merrill, R. M., Aldana, S. G., Pope, J. E., Anderson, D. R., Coberley, C. R., Grossmeier, J. J., & Whitmer, R. W. (2013). Self-Rated Job Performance and Absenteeism According to Employee Engagement, Health Behaviors, and Physical Health. *Journal of Occupational and Environmental Medicine*, 55, 10–18.

O'Driscoll, M. P. (1996). The Interface Between Job and Off-Job Roles: Enhancement and Conflict. *International Review of Industrial and Organizational Psychology*, 11, 279–306.

Palmer, S., & Cooper, C. L. (2007). How to Deal With Stress. *The Sunday Times*. London & Philadelphia: Kogan Page.

Sainsbury Centre for Mental Health. (2007). *Mental Health at Work: Developing the Business Case*. Policy Paper 8. Sainsbury Centre for Mental Health, London.

Williams, S., & Cooper, C. L. (1998). Measuring Occupational Stress: Development of the Pressure Management Indicator. *Journal of Occupational Health Psychology*, 3, 306–321.

6 Becoming a Spartan W@rker

How do you dream of yourself? How do you imagine your future in the business industry? Do you want to look like the majority, just waiting for the time to pass by patiently to return back home and thinking that you do not want to go to work the next day? If your answer is yes and if you feel good with that, it seems that you will remain in your comfort zone, which it is perfectly fine to us since it is OK to you.

Most probably, though, and since you have decided to obtain this book, it seems that you want something more for yourself; it seems that you have an eagerness to get out of your comfort zone and face life directly.

In this chapter we are going to blend the features of Spartan warriors with the current trends and difficulties of the modern work environment and life in general, with the aim to devise a new employee prototype. Devising such a new prototype of individuals, who distinguish themselves from other people based on the skills that they possess, will eventually lead such individuals to elevate themselves when compared to others and become what we call Spartan W@rkers.

Where do you stand?

Before we proceed forward to this chapter, let us define what a Spartan W@rker really means:

A Spartan W@rker is an individual who has the ability to overcome and recover quickly from any form of adversity, illness, hardship or significant source of stress. Such individuals can be characterized as strong, tough, hardy and adaptable to change. A Spartan W@rker does not reflect a sum of traits that an individual either possesses or does not. On the contrary, becoming a Spartan W@rker means that one should engage in a number of behaviours, thoughts and actions which can be learned and developed by anyone who is willing to invest to the growth of the self. However, we need to notice here that the image of a Spartan W@rker is not that of a person who does not experience difficulties or distress in everyday life. Emotional discomfort and pain are also parts of the equation for individuals who are willing to become highly resilient and manage stress effectively. This occurs because, in order to become a Spartan W@rker, you need to fight your way into the stress arena and develop your skills through experience and learning.

Now that we have defined what a Spartan W@rker is and what characteristics one should possess for becoming a Spartan W@rker, the question that arises is the following:

Where do you begin?

Well, it is true that the development of resilience is a personal quest. Not all people share the same personality traits and life experiences. For this reason, there are a number of personality assessments that help individuals figure out their psychological profile, with the aim to become aware of both their strengths and weaknesses that need to change. In other words, one must map the internal self in order to build the existing individual portrait and then gradually start painting the new portrait of the person who is willing to become.

Below we are going to propose some specific psychometric tests that will help you map your current status, but feel free to use any instrument that has been scientifically proved to be reliable and valid in the assessment of personality, levels of stress and levels of resilience.

The Five Factor Model (FFM)

One influential and widely used tool that can provide you with some really valuable information is the Five Factor Model of personality (FFM; Costa & MacCrae, 1992). The FFM measure the five dimensions of personality. These dimensions can map the inner 'OCEAN' of one's self, since one's personality can be characterized as vast and multidimensional:

- Openness to new experiences
- Conscientiousness
- Extraversion
- Agreeableness
- Neuroticism

Moreover, each of these dimensions comprises six subscales that analyze more in depth the traits of one's personality. For instance, and in relation to our theme and values of Spartan W@rker, openness to new experience includes, among other subscales, 'Actions and Values'; conscientiousness includes, among other subscales, 'Achievement Striving and Self-Discipline'; extra-version includes, among other subscales, 'Excitement Seeking and Positive Emotions'; agreeableness includes, among other subscales, 'Trust and Modesty'; and neuroticism includes, among other subscales, 'Impulsiveness, Depression and Vulnerability to Stress'.

All of these subscales involve characteristics that define your current state in terms of the qualities needed to become a Spartan W@rker. It does not really matter where you stand now – what really matters is that you are familiar with your own strengths and weaknesses and, based on these assumptions, you can decide on your new action plan.

i-resilience

Throughout the first chapters we have introduced and defined the term resilience. In this section we are going to analyze further the theory behind resilience, its characteristics and its benefits for the individual. It is very interesting to know that although personality characteristics are more stable during adulthood, the capacity to improve and increase levels of resilience is not. No matter the existing level, resilience can be developed and can protect general wellbeing from everyday stressors.

This is the reason of why RobertsonCooper Ltd created the i-resilience report. The i-resilience report is a free online self-assessment inventory that informs you about your current levels of resilience (www.robertsoncooper.com/our-products/i-resilience-free-report). On the one hand, the i-resilience report offers valuable information about the personality characteristics (based on the FFM theory) and skills that are necessary for individuals to possess when they come to deal with demanding work situations. On the other hand, it makes suggestions on your strong points and how you can take advantage of them, while at the same time it highlights the areas that hinder your resilience levels and makes suggestions on how to improve them. Basically, i-resilience can be used as a naval compass that informs you about which areas of yourself need change so as to increase your resilience levels even more, protecting your overall wellbeing and helping you thrive in your work context. The resilient philosophy is not a new idea and implies the capability of individuals to maintain enhanced levels of performance and physical/psychological wellbeing under overwhelming situations, while at the same time being able to bounce back and adjust easily to hardship or change. Resilience means never to give up. As the Spartans, before each battle, used to say: *i tan i epi tas*, which means either you come back with your shield as a winner or dead upon it!

In more recent times Nelson Mandela said: 'The greatest glory in living lies not in never falling, but in rising every time we fall.'

Components of resilience

The key components of resilience are:

1 Social support
2 Purposefulness
3 Confidence
4 Adaptability.

By increasing your resilience, you increase as described by the initial letters, what we call your SPartan CApability. Let's elaborate on that by further discussing each component separately. When it comes to social support, the Spartan W@rker is able to form constructive, meaningful and strategic relationships because he/she understands that seeking support from others during difficult situations is more efficient and less stressful compared to when someone has to cope with the adversities alone. Spartan warriors fought always as a cohesive team, with the shield of each Spartan protecting his fellow warrior during battle. That is why a small number of Spartans could easily confront higher numbers of enemy troops during battle, because they were synchronizing to work as a team, as a single entity with the same goals, motives, fears and aspirations. Such unity made even the impossible appear possible. The same stands for the Spartan W@rker and the modern work environment, where a well-formed and cohesive team can manage difficult and demanding projects with ease and minimum discomfort even when external factors are pressing.

Purposefulness constitutes another key feature of the Spartan W@rker. One must have a clear purpose in life. Purpose is the energy that makes you move forward during turbulent times. A strong purpose based on values makes someone persistent and determined to successfully achieve any goal, regardless of the resulting costs. Spartans had a strong willingness to excel in everything they were up to, from training, to battle, to singing, to dancing, to sports, to the upbringing of the best citizens for a state. Their purpose for life was based in the propagation of the common good and in the progress of their nation – surely strong values for that time, values that we can parallel with our current work environments, families and friends. Do not deceive yourself: our reality, characterized by such an economic unrest and insecurity, looks like a battle terrain nowadays into which we enter every day and for which we need to possess and improve specific skills in order to succeed and survive. And this is why we need to have a clear purpose of where we want to arrive and through which methods we can achieve this. Sometimes we might deviate from our way, but this is normal. We reboot ourselves and our resources and we return back to battle once again. The interesting point is that when we have a purpose we experience pleasure, satisfaction and eagerness to begin the day, whereas when we do not have a purpose, we just rush through the day in a repetitive pattern, letting our lives pass without a cause, which in turns results in the manifestation of feelings of distress and emptiness.

Confidence is a core feature of capability. If you do not possess self-confidence or self-efficacy (Bandura, 1997), you will always make circles around the same identical point where you stand right now without taking initiatives and without succeeding at anything in life. Spartan W@rkers embrace feelings of competence – even in the face of novel situations and challenges – that they will manage to complete the task successfully, overcoming the obstacles and achieving their goals. One must possess high levels of self-esteem to be able to effectively manage stressful situations no matter the odds. One might even fail, but even if this is the case, one will become stronger and wiser from such experience and eventually will make use of such knowledge in the future. Spartan warriors considered themselves as highly confident and capable human beings, even in the face of death, and that is why, when needed, 300 of them stood against the whole army of the Persian Empire. Did they have any likelihood to succeed? Did they have any chance? But did it really matter for them? No . . . they were confident about their skills, while at the same time they had a purpose in their ancient life. If it was to die, they preferred dying gloriously in battle, fighting for freedom, to hiding in the shadows and living enslaved. Spartans managed to do so because they had developed highly resilient skills for their time, as we have seen in the first chapters of the book. In order to do so, they were tailored always towards the cultivation and experience of positive emotions, which are considered essential features for one's resilience levels, instead of living in negativity. We should follow their example in life.

Adaptability is of paramount importance. To understand that, let's elaborate on an example taking under consideration the components of resilience presented so far. You have a strong 'purpose' and willingness to achieve a business idea so you start making plans and improvising ways to move forward. You are 'confident' enough that you can manage the project all the way, coping with any difficulty or discomfort. All this energy that you have is inspiring, and you draw the attention of individuals who are like you and want to be part of your vision, your purpose to serve the society. You have built your 'social support' network, and you rush towards your goal completion. Everything looks good up to here, but what if you are not 'adaptable' to change? What if you cannot recover easily from your setbacks and roadblocks? Well, without adaptability you are not going anywhere. Without the ability and flexibility to adapt to demanding conditions and uncontrollable changes you cannot move forward. You need to possess a sense of internal locus of control (Rotter, 1966) that, no matter what, you can influence what is happening in your life and you can always find ways to overcome problems and create new solutions and pathways. The control of life lies within you and is not susceptible to external factors such as luck or fate.

Psychological hardiness

Another influential theoretical framework of the occupational stress literature that provides a route towards resilience is psychological hardiness (Kobasa, 1979), which asserts that 'hardy' individuals are more resilient to stress. This model presents the three 'Cs' of a hardy personality, which stand for the following:

- Control
- Commitment
- Challenge.

According to Kobasa (1979), hardy individuals can exert some control over life events, thus directly influencing their life outcomes; are committed to the activities and the goals that they undertake; and perceive difficult situations more as a challenge rather as a threat, since they consider learning from life experiences (either positive or negative) to be of paramount importance for their development. These characteristics can be cultivated, and in turn it is the cultivation of these skills that keep individuals healthy when confronted with demanding and stressful conditions (Kobasa, Maddi & Kahn, 1982). Through the development of these '3Cs', Spartan W@rkers derive the constant courage and motivation needed to focus on difficult and seemingly impossible work tasks, turning stressful and unmanageable conditions into opportunities for immense growth and progress. Another strong link between resilience and psychological hardiness lies in the later addition of a fourth 'C' in the equation, that of closeness, which is a form of social support that involves the mutual giving and taking of help and support, and which in turns gives raise to the occurrence of a number of positive effects for the individual, such as the experience of less occupational stress and higher job satisfaction (Maddi, 1999).

Mental toughness

Another term that should be embraced by individuals who are aiming to increase their resilient levels is that of 'mental toughness'. The concept of mental toughness has been used extensively in the world of sports, but obviously it has also been linked to the business world for a number of reasons.

According to Clough, Earle and Sewell (2002, p. 38): 'Mentally Tough individuals have a high sense of self-belief and an unshakable faith that they control their own destiny, these individuals can remain relatively unaffected by competition and adversity.' Researchers have reported a positive relationship between mental toughness and a number of factors related to resilience, such as feelings of optimism, the ability to better cope with stressful conditions, the ability to perform efficiently under pressure and the ability to confront problems directly instead of avoiding them (Nicholls, Polman, Levy & Backhouse, 2008). Actually, mental toughness theory shares similar characteristics with psychological hardiness, and this can be seen through an examination of the items of the Mental Toughness Questionnaire 48 (MTQ48; Clough, Earle & Sewell, 2002), which is based on the '4Cs' model and its subcomponents:

- Control: Refers to the experienced emotions and the influence that individuals can exert over life events.
- Commitment: The inclination to be totally devoted and involved in all activities and projects undertaken.
- Challenge: The understanding that life is unpredictable and prone to change and the ability to view demanding conditions as opportunities for growth and not as threats.
- Confidence: Refers to one's abilities to manage demanding conditions and to succeed, as well as to one's interpersonal skills to form strong support networks.

As stated previously, the concept of mental toughness, although it has flourished in sports, also has received high acceptance in the business world due to the fact that both in sports and business, people come to face and deal with similar demanding conditions and challenges. Being mentally tough and resilient is a factor of paramount importance for success and personal growth. The lives of employees who strive for success can be paralleled with those of athletes and with those who serve in military Special Forces units, each one in a different specialty. There is an obvious link between all those who are willing to play in the elite division, either in business, sports or the military.

Emotional intelligence

Until now we have presented the theoretical perspectives of four influential models, namely the Five Factor Model, resilience, psychological hardiness and mental toughness. It is very interesting to notice that all these models and theories related to personal development, resilience and stress management share a certain number of common characteristics. Let's elaborate on that as we discuss another important framework, namely Goleman's Emotional Intelligence (EI, 1995). Emotional intelligence is defined as the internal ability to recognize, regulate and express one's emotions and being able to comprehend others' emotions so as to handle interpersonal relationships in a better and more empathetic way. Goleman contends that emotional intelligence should not be considered as the sum of static personality traits but rather can be cultivated and developed to such an extent that it can act as a contributory factor for both personal and professional success and overall wellbeing. The four core elements of EI theory are the following, and each one includes a number of subdivisions that are illustrated here:

1 Self-awareness: The ability to understand one's internal state, desires and available resources:

   • Emotional self-awareness
   • Accurate self-assessment
   • Self-confidence

2 Self-management: The ability to manage one's internal state, desires and available resources:

   • Emotional self-control
   • Trustworthiness
   • Conscientiousness
   • Adaptability
   • Achievement drive
   • Initiative

3 Social awareness: The ability to handle interpersonal relationships effectively:

   • Empathy
   • Organizational awareness
   • Service orientation

4 Social skills: The ability to stimulate desirable responses in others:

   • Developing others
   • Influence
   • Communication
   • Conflict management
   • Visionary leadership
   • Catalyzing change
   • Building bonds
   • Teamwork and collaboration

Relating to our comment that all models that we have presented so far share certain characteristics between them and that their primary goal is that of protecting one's overall wellbeing and fostering one's personal development and resilience levels, we propose that the blend of all these features are of paramount importance for anyone who wants to become a Spartan W@rker.

Comparing the emotional intelligence competencies with the traits of the Five Factor Model (FFM) of personality (Costa & MacCrae, 1992), one can find many similarities. For instance, we can assume that the 'Extraversion' scale of the FFM shares some common characteristics with influence, communication, visionary leadership, building bonds and teamwork and collaboration from the 'Social skills' scale. Furthermore, we can assume that openness to experience and conscientiousness share some common characteristics with initiative and with conscientiousness and achievement driving, respectively, from the 'Self-management' scale. Agreeableness can be paralleled with the 'Social awareness' scale, since agreeableness is characterized by a sense of empathy and consideration towards others, which is a subscale in the 'Social awareness' scale. Finally, in terms of the 'Self-awareness' scale, it seems that there is no direct link with the FFM.

Likewise, a number of correlations were reported between resilience and the FFM. More specifically, researchers reported a negative correlation between resilience and the dimension of neuroticism, with neurotic individuals reporting low resilience levels. On the contrary, significant positive relationships were observed between resilience and the dimension of extraversion, as well as between resilience and the dimension of 'openness to experience' (Fredrickson, Tugade, Waugh & Larkin, 2003).

Following the same frame of reasoning, we can observe many similarities between the models that lead towards resilience as illustrated in Table 6.1. What we attempt to propose here is that the core idea and approach remain the same, that of always aiming to cultivate strong skills that will empower you towards completion of your goals, no matter what these goals are, either for optimum health, work outcomes, personal relationships etc.

Table 6.1 Similarities between models

Resilience	Psychological hardiness	Mental toughness	Emotional intelligence
Adaptability	Control	Control	Self-management
Purposefulness	Commitment	Commitment	Self-awareness
Confidence	Challenge	Challenge	Social awareness
Social support	Closeness	Confidence	Social skills

As shown in the table, the Resilience–Adaptability scale (the flexibility of an individual to adapt to changes and overcome obstacles) is met also as a subscale, again under the title Adaptability, in the Self-management scale of 'Emotional intelligence'. In addition, one can argue that an individual who scores high in Adaptability possess a strong sense of self-control, meaning that individuals can constructively and adaptively control their responses to demanding situations. Control is a core element of both models of 'Psychological hardiness' and 'Mental toughness' and is also met as a subscale in the Self-management scale of 'Emotional intelligence', namely Self-control, which is defined as the ability to keep negative emotions and impulses under control.

The Resilience–Purposefulness scale (the existence of a clear purpose and values that internally drive an individual forward to surpass any setback) can also be linked to the Commitment scale of both the 'Psychological hardiness' and 'Mental toughness' models. In order to succeed in any given situation, you must have a high sense of purpose and clear goals and you must be committed in everything you do. Through strong purpose and commitment, one can remain engaged and motivated, thus reaching high achievement and performance levels.

The Resilience–Confidence scale (an individual's strong feelings of self-competence, self-worth and capability) is also met as the fourth 'C' in the 'Mental toughness' model, and likewise it exists as a subscale in the Self-awareness scale of 'Emotional intelligence', namely Self-confidence. As discussed in the beginning of this chapter when we introduced the concept of resilience, it appears that only when you possess enough self-confidence and high levels of self-esteem can you achieve your goals and become highly resilient when confronting difficult situations.

The Resilience–Social support scale (the ability to build and maintain positive and strong relationships with others, which can support an individual during times of crisis) is also included in the 'Psychological hardiness' model with the Closeness scale, and additionally in two scales in the 'Emotional intelligence' model, namely 'Social awareness' (subscale Empathy) and 'Social skills' (e.g. subscales 'Teamwork and cooperation', 'Building bonds'). We have outlined throughout the book the importance of teamwork for both work success and personal resilience. We humans prefer to interact and operate within social networks. This is also a reason why the majority of us prefer to live in cities where millions of people are interacting daily. We feel safer when we belong to subgroups of people either at work or in our personal relationships; it comes naturally for us, and we can perform and manage life easier. It always feels nice when you know that you have people around you who you can count on in difficult situations, and it also feels nice when you help somebody else under the same spectrum.

ASSET

Now let's focus on your work environment. If we blend the above models with ASSET we can gain a clear picture of our personality profile (strengths and weaknesses), of our resilience levels and stress management skills, and finally of the most critical occupational stressors that negatively affect our physical health, psychological wellbeing and productivity levels. Most probably, up to this point you will have completed the free i-resilience test. If you have not, please do so before reading any further. Go to the following link, run the test and receive your report, which you can use as a starting point:

www.robertsoncooper.com/our-products/i-resilience-free-report

Going back to ASSET: ASSET is a tool that is used to measure employees' wellbeing in any given work environment as well as to examine which characteristics of the workplace may have a positive or negative impact on you. The way through which we perceive situations at work, either as stressful or not, is significantly influenced by our personalities and the overall attitude (positive or negative) that we tend to hold, and consequently these characteristics influence our coping effectiveness in every situation. The work environment is in fact a complex one, involving several situations that we have to deal with throughout the day. These work situations continuously test our resilience, and of course it is through these situations that we learn and develop our resilience levels. So we propose that at moments where others might get overwhelmed by a situation, you must view it as a chance to learn a new skill, while at the same time you can increase your ability to be resilient. It really does not matter if you succeed or not; it only matters that you got out of your comfort zone.

ASSET explores the following work situations, and for each one we give an example of what skills you need to develop in order to manage your work environment more efficiently, become more resilient and protect your overall health and productivity levels:

- Work relationships: Aim to cultivate your interpersonal and social skills so as to be able to develop collaborative, constructive and meaningful relationships at work. Use this work social support network when needed to manage highly demanding and stressful conditions at work.
- Work–life balance: Try to organize your work obligations and your time management so as not to bring work home and, most importantly, to maintain low levels of work stress, which means that stress will not affect your personal life.

- Overload: Aim always to improve the way you perform your duties, involve others in the process so as to share the work burden and try to say no when someone is giving you more work than what you can manage at this particular time period.
- Job security: Aim to always develop your skills and your ability, and you will feel less stressed and feel more secure in your workplace, since you will become a valuable asset for your organization and your colleagues. Also learn to adjust and manage changes more effectively, and you will save yourself from the experience of unnecessary discomfort.
- Control: Always protect and increase your levels of job control. Ask your supervisor to delegate to you the responsibility of projects and follow your own way of doing things, the way that makes you feel more comfortable. Always do the same towards your colleagues, and through this combination you will see highly stressful demands be managed easily.
- Resources and communication: Try to be updated with all the new developments in your line of business. Being well informed will save you from surprises and also will help you to perform your duties more adequately. Always ask for the resources needed to do your job. You cannot scan a document if you do not have a printer, so ask for one.
- Pay and benefits: Since we offer our time and skills to an organization, we expect to be compensated accordingly through pay and benefits. Regardless of the nature of your job, always try to perform every task, from the simplest to the most complex, in the best possible way, and then believe us that you will not even have to ask for a raise: they will give it to you to keep you happy, motivated and satisfied.
- Aspects of the job: Try to avoid dull and repetitive work. Always try to be involved in challenging projects that will boost your career. Boredom at work can be catastrophic, so choose work environments or job posts that will keep you stimulated and engaged in your work. When working you need to be part of a higher cause, you need to have a meaning and, as discussed in the resilience model, you need to have a purpose and a clear goal that will make you increase your job satisfaction.

Where is the link?

Some of you may wonder if it is possible that a linkage exists between the ancient Spartans and the humans of our time in everyday life. Well, it is not a secret that concepts such as resilience, hardiness and mental toughness also have been developed through military research programs in an effort to create strong cohesive units that can operate well and for prolonged periods with the minimum discomfort and distress. Researchers wanted to assess what the characteristics were that made certain people succeed in Special Forces training, and they found that hardy and resilient individuals were more successful in completing the training and could endure the harsh military life more easily when compared to less hardy and resilient individuals (Bartone, 1995). Resilience training in the US military is considered mandatory from 2008, when Professor Martin Seligman was requested by the US military authority to create a complete resilience program that would promote the psychological fitness of all military personnel and their families during periods of prolonged deployments and stressful conditions. By September 2010, more than 800,000 people had completed the resilience assessment (Seligman, 2011). The complete Master Resilience Training (MRT) program included training on resilience (e.g. self-regulation, mental agility), mental toughness (e.g. energy management, reducing catastrophic thinking), identifying character strengths (e.g. individual and team strengths, use of strengths to overcome obstacles), sustainment (promoting prolonged development of resilience for forthcoming years to preserve the wellbeing of military personnel) and enhancement (e.g. mental skills development, increase of self-confidence) (Reivich, Seligman & McBride, 2011).

It is reasonable to think that resilience and mental toughness training could be successfully applied to the modern work environment, because if you consider it, one can parallel the modern work environment with a 'war terrain', and in this war terrain the levels of stress experienced are extremely high and need to be controlled. Although each environment faces different occupational stressors, all stressors, no matter if we are discussing employees, athletes or soldiers, can negatively affect both their physical and psychological wellbeing. Some individuals will become overstressed a lot in the same situations where others will feel and act normally as if no pressure exists. Hence, one can understand why the Spartans had developed such an effective upbringing system that promoted resilience, hardiness and mental toughness in all aspects of social life, including military, sports, family and social activities, and with very positive results. And it was these results that made this particular group of people praiseworthy even 2,500 years later and to be used as an example when discussing topics of mental and physical strength, pride, courage, commitment and sacrifice for the good of others, all characteristics of the resilient and hardy individual. These are the characteristics and the philosophy that we would like you to embrace in your everyday lifestyle. By doing so you are going to take part in the most interesting and stimulating project of your life: To become a better and more complete you.

Resilience is an effort to reach homeostasis, the capability of maintaining a constant point of equilibrium, but in order to achieve that, one must adopt a more holistic philosophy about life and stress. One must understand that in order to become a Spartan W@rker, you will do so by developing and flourishing through adversities and difficulties in life. So if you have taken a decision to follow the path of the Spartan W@rker, you must be ready to confront and test yourself in order to see what material you are made of. What everyone must comprehend is that in order to effectively build resilience one must (Bonanno, 2004):

1 Be aware of the fact that resilience is not something alien to us; rather, it is an internal mechanism that, if cultivated properly, will keep us healthy during distressing moments.
2 Realize that through resilience one can maintain a healthy everyday functioning when dealing with adversities and also promote personal growth, development and the use of positive emotions.
3 Accept that there is no one specific route towards resilience; rather there are many ways through which one can enrich himself/herself with resilient skills, always based upon each individual's unique features and lifestyle.

To conclude, what you need to know in terms of resilience, which will help you in your journey to become a Spartan W@rker, is that concepts such as resilience, hardiness, mental toughness and emotional intelligence:

• Can be learned, and you only have to possess a positive attitude towards constructive change and towards new experiences in life;
• Can be reached by everyone, not somewhere around you, but in your grasp, within yourself;
• Can combine all learned skills, where learned skills can be used with a cumulative effect in the combat against stress. The more skills you learn, the higher your ability to confront difficult and demanding situations; and
• Can start right now from where you stand, meaning your current levels of resilience.

You must keep in mind that through reading this book so far you have already triggered and formed new neural pathways towards resilience and stress management at work and everyday life. We are entering an era of what specialists call the 'super brain'. The human brain is considered to be one of the most complex and unique systems of our universe. Scientists even view the brain as 'the three pound universe' (Chopra & Tanzi, 2012). The latest research suggests that our brain capabilities are enormous and that, as with every other organ in our body, in order to stay sharp, we must feed it and nurture it, we must take advantage of what is called neuroplasticity. Neuroplasticity is the ability of the brain to restructure itself and its functions through the creation of new neural pathways during a lifetime, responding actively to new experiences and to stimuli originating from the external environment. Interestingly, the nutrients desired from our brain in order to keep it fit are nothing more than stimulants. By stimulants we mean the exposure of ourselves to new experiences and to the development of new skills (Chopra & Tanzi, 2012). It does not matter what these experiences and skills are; the aim is to keep the brain active. You can play chess, do gardening, go for a walk, start a new sport or practice public speaking skills for work purposes, and you still trigger and create new and strong neural pathways in your brain. Now imagine the effect that this will have in your brain if you consciously focus and engage in a number of activities that will enhance your resilience. It will most probably create a whole new brain, ready to deal with every obstacle that you encounter in your way. Remember that even by thinking about it as you read through these lines you are already creating a new schema in your brain that you can label as resilience. After that, you just need to nurture it. To make it simple, imagine it as a thin thread that connects two neurons in your brain. It might not seem like that much, but it is a start. It is up to you on whether you will leave it as it is or nurture it and create a whole network of threads that are creating connections between millions of neurons, thus developing massively your levels of resilience.

Summary

From all this one can understand that the route towards resilience and well-being contains certain universal characteristics that are accepted from many researchers and are well established in the literature. Another very important characteristic is that all researchers indicate that these skills can be learned and can be developed no matter your current status. So by developing the aforementioned skills that are collectively presented in Table 6.1, one can become more resilient, more 'hardy', more mentally tough and more emotionally intelligent throughout life. These are the skills that we are going to elaborate on in the next two chapters of this book. By developing these skills, one can become a Spartan W@rker, with the word Spartan referring to individuals who embrace the following characteristics:

• Strong
• Persistent
• Adaptable
• Resilient
• Tough

- Able
- Noble.

Please invest two more minutes of your time to reread these words, but this time try to refer them to yourself. For instance: 'I am strong, I am persistent, I am adaptable' and so on. How does it feel? Does it come naturally when you express these words towards yourself? Do you believe that you are all of the above, some of the above or none of the above? You need to understand that every single thought and action stems from your mind and from your mentality towards change. Try to reward yourself by stating these expressions every day when you wake up. After a while, you will understand that these phrases will work as a boosting mechanism in the beginning of your day.

References

Bandura, A. (1997). *Self-Efficacy: The Exercise of Control*. New York, US: Freeman/Times Books/Henry Holt & Co.

Bartone, P. T. (1995). *A Short Hardiness Scale*. Paper Presented at (July 1995). Meeting of the American Psychological Society, New York.

Bonanno, G. A. (2004). Loss, Trauma, and Human Resilience: Have We Under-Estimated the Human Capacity to Thrive After Extremely Adverse Events? *American Psychologist*, 59, 20–28.

Chopra, D., & Tanzi, R. E. (2012). *Super Brain: Unleashing the Explosive Power of Your Mind to Maximize Health, Happiness and Spiritual Well-Being*. New York: Random House.

Clough, P. J., Earle, K., & Sewell, D. F. (2002). Mental Toughness: The Concept and Its Measurement. In I. Cockerill (Ed.), *Solutions in Sport Psychology* (pp. 32–47). London: Thompson.

Costa, P. T., & MacCrae, R. R. (1992). *Revised NEO Personality Inventory (NEO PI-R) and NEO Five-Factor Inventory (NEO FFI) Manual*. Odessa, FL: Psychological Assessment Resources.

Fredrickson, B. L., Tugade, M. M., Waugh, C. E., & Larkin, G. R. (2003). What Good Are Positive Emotions in Crisis? A Prospective Study of Resilience and Emotions Following the Terrorist Attacks on the United States on September 11th, 2001. *Journal of Personality and Social Psychology*, 84, 365–376.

Goleman, D. (1995). *Emotional Intelligence*. New York: Bantam.

Kobasa, S. C. (1979). Stressful Life Events, Personality, and Health: An Inquiry Into Hardiness. *Journal of Personality and Social Psychology*, 37, 1–11.

Kobasa, S. C., Maddi, S. R., & Kahn, S. (1982). Hardiness and Health: A Prospective Study. *Journal of Personality and Social Psychology*, 42, 168–177.

Maddi, S. R. (1999). Comments on Trends in Hardiness Research and Theorizing. *Consulting Psychology Journal*, 51, 67–71.

Nicholls, A. R., Polman, R. C. J., Levy, A. R., & Backhouse, S. H. (2008). Mental Toughness, Optimism, Pessimism, and Coping Among Athletes. *Personality and Individual Differences*, 44, 1182–1192.

Quotery. Retrieved 24th October 2016: http://www.quotery.com/quotes/the-greatest-glory-in-living-lies-not-in-never-falling/

Reivich, K., Seligman, M., & McBride, S. (2011). Master Resilience Training in the US Army. *American Psychologist*, 66, 25–34.

RobertsonCooper Ltd. Retrieved 18th September 2016: www.robertsoncooper.com/our-products/i-resilience-free-report

Rotter, J. B. (1966). Generalized Expectancies for Internal Versus External Control of Reinforcement. *Psychological Monographs*, 80, 1–28.

Seligman, M. (2011). *Flourish: A Visionary New Understanding of Happiness and Well-Being*. New York: Free Press.

7 The Spartan W@rker's coping techniques

In this chapter a presentation of various coping strategies and techniques that will help you to deal effectively with stress and to increase your resilience levels is made. There are many techniques that individuals can use to enhance their resilience and to manage stress appropriately both in the work environment and in their personal lives. However, it is worthwhile to mention at this point that each individual, through past experience and learning, possesses a different and unique set of resilient characteristics upon which they rely, when needed.

Hence, it is important to understand that in order to develop supreme levels of resilience and to advance yourself in becoming a Spartan W@ rker, you have to take individual responsibility for your actions and efforts, always keeping in mind that if you succeed, every aspect of your life will be improved too. The techniques that will be presented to you are not only applicable in your workplace – even though they are devised to make you stronger in your everyday work interactions – but they can also be applied in your personal life, as well. For this reason, the content of our examples is not specifically tailored towards your work, but it rather contains an explanation of the benefits that such techniques offer to your overall wellbeing.

Before we begin, let's briefly demonstrate the significance of coping in the battle against stress. As seen in Figure 7.1, between the potential work stressors and the eventual negative expression of stress (physical, psychological or behavioural) lies the individual with his or her unique characteristics.

This approach is similar to Selye's (1956) stress model (Chapter 3). The demands of the work environment (and of life in general) are called stressors and constitute significant sources of stress for the individual. Stressors are perceived by the individual either as threatening or not and are dealt with according to each individual's unique set of coping skills.

But what is the definition of coping? 'Coping consists of cognitive and behavioural efforts to manage specific external and/or internal demands that

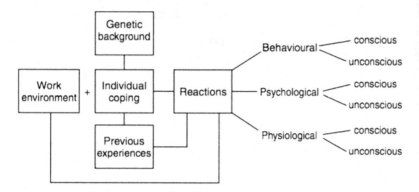

Figure 7.1 Theoretical model of the interaction between the environment, the individual, and his or her reactions

Source: Adapted from Kagan & Levi (1971).

are appraised as taxing or exceeding the resources of the person' (Folkman & Lazarus, 1991, p. 210). Through this definition one can understand the following:

- Coping is an active process where the individual reacts cognitively and behaviourally in certain ways while confronting a demanding situation in order to manage psychological stress.
- Coping involves the reaction of the person to environmental factors that disturb homeostasis and tax or exceed the individual's resources.
- Coping refers to the individuals' appraisal of the situation.
- Coping depends on the availability of resources.
- The coping process and the development of effective coping skills require substantial effort by the individual.

Coping effectiveness is the result of the combination of genes, previous learning and the availability of individual coping skills (the more coping skills, the better). These elements are responsible for individuals' reactions towards stressors. If coping is satisfactory, then the levels of stress remain low, and therefore the individual does not experience any discomfort. But if coping is inadequate, then the individual cannot adapt to the pressure, reacts negatively and manifests various physical, psychological and behavioural symptoms (Lazarus & Folkman, 1984).

As you can see in Figure 7.1, there is a constant feedback between reaction and work stressors. If coping was successful, then the coping skills are enriched and upgraded, thus meaning that if the individual will have to deal with the same or a similar stressor in the future, the stressor will be dealt with more easily and effectively. On the opposite side, if the coping intervention was not successful, then the feedback suggests that next time alternative coping techniques must be used to deal with the stressor. Although the negative experience of stress was not prevented in this occasion, which can often be the case and is perfectly fine, the individual can benefit by using this outcome constructively and has the chance to gain precious knowledge for future reference. For instance, while you are giving a public speech at work, you might get stuck during the speech in some difficult phrases, resulting in you feeling stressed, sweating and losing your flow. You can learn through this negative experience, and at your next public event you can rehearse adequately on difficult phrases, so as to avoid such a negative experience in the future by being better prepared.

A frequent question that might arise in your mind is where do we start from? The theory is good, but how do we move forward? You must always bear in mind that great changes happen over time, so you need to set small and methodical goals to reach your objective. You need to be patient and consistent. Putting it into a philosophical perspective, you need to embrace the principles of Kaizen, which suggest that a person should make small steps towards progress every day. Kaizen is a Japanese concept that focuses on attention to detail and on the continuous improvement of every aspect of life (Maurer, 2004). Change does not happen overnight, so you will have to take it slowly in order to experience solid and long-lasting results and overcome the instinctual fear of change (Maurer, 2004). For example, if you want to write an important project proposal at work, but every five minutes you avoid writing by distracting yourself with irrelevant tasks due to your fears that your proposal will not be good enough and no one will appreciate it, you will never finish writing. Therefore, small actions and small commitments like writing a paragraph every time you sit on your desk will nurture and motivate your brain to find ways to overcome any roadblock, making the achievement of this goal more possible to occur.

Essentially, you need to do the following:

- Think big on what you want to achieve in terms of resilience and stress management.
- Start small in terms of the tasks that you will do.
- Start now. Not tomorrow, not Monday, NOW.

Please feel free to choose any of the coping techniques that we propose, the one that fits easier to your everyday life, and go for it. Choose a technique that seems more appropriate for you, a technique that will help you to overcome a difficult situation at once. If you achieve that, then you are already there. You are on track, and you have added another weapon in your armoury against stress and towards a more fulfilling life.

Now take a moment to reflect on your success. Reflect on each of your achievements, no matter how small or big they are. Feel proud of your accomplishment and tend to use that as an exemplar when, at some point in the future, you will want to boost your efforts.

For instance, you might wish to improve your physical condition, so you decide that:

> I want to increase my levels of physical exercise in order to become healthier and lose some extra pounds; therefore two days per week I will go for a 20-minute walk in the neighbourhood before I go to work.

If you attempt to do that the following morning, then you introduce your brain to a new habit and a new skill that will improve your resilience. Although this initially might appear to be a small thing to you, do not forget that it is a start, especially when we are referring to action. By doing so, you show commitment to change and you feel satisfied with yourself. At this precise moment you need to set some SMART goals towards resilience. With the word SMART we mean that your goals (we will use the previously mentioned example in the following analysis) must be:

- Specific: You do not say that 'I will start doing more physical exercise', rather you try to be as specific as possible by answering the five 'W' questions – *what* do I want to achieve (I want to improve my physical condition), *why* do I want to do that (to become healthier and lose some extra pounds), *who* will be involved (me), *where* will this happen (in the neighbourhood) and *which* are the details (go for walking, two days per week, 20 minutes, before I go to work).
- Measurable: It is crucial for your goals to be measurable and not vague in order to monitor your performance and keep yourself motivated throughout the journey. When you state that you will walk for 20 minutes two days per week, you are putting in place a measure that will help you monitor your progress. For instance, assume that the first week you have walked 15 minutes for two days, so you are close to the achievement of your initial goal, and you feel excited and eager to reach the 20-minute goal the following week.
- Achievable: For a goal to be valid it should be within your abilities. It is not reasonable to state that you will walk for two hours at once if you have not done this before. Most likely this goal will never be reached, your enthusiasm will be lost and your motivation will be decreased.

- Realistic: It is important that your goal is stimulating and stretching, but it should be realistic and relevant to your lifestyle and within your control. You might state that you want to go for walking before you go to work, but what if your work is one hour away and you need to be there at 8:00 am? Is it realistic for you to wake up at 6:00 am, or will you overstretch yourself? This is relevant, and of course is case specific and depends on each individual's general lifestyle. Remember that what might be feasible for you might not be feasible for someone else, and vice versa.
- Time-bound: There must be a deadline for each goal. You might desire to lose these extra pounds, but if you do not set a time interval, for example, let's say a period of two months, it is easier to get carried away and eventually to let the goal vanish. It is useful to set some short-term milestones as you move forward that will assist you in measuring your progress.

How do you measure progress and keep on track?

When you decide to begin this journey of cultivating individual resilience, you should organize yourself as much as possible. For each goal you set that aims to develop any of the coping strategies that lie under the philosophy of Spartan W@rker, you need to have a specific plan. Spartans in their upbringing system – *agoge* – were very careful in the way in which they were rearing their offspring since their early years of age (age 5) in order to create the best citizens for the state. Of course, we do not suggest that you should arrive at such extremes, but as they successfully did so many centuries ago, it is important to understand the necessity of proper organization if you wish to reap the benefits at both your work environment and personal life.

For example, as a disciplined Spartan W@rker, you would set some long-term goals, lasting probably two to three months, and would also do some performance-review cycles along the way to check up on your progress, so as to help you review your techniques to enhance your performance. We understand that one of the most common problems of the modern individual is time availability, so you need to keep the reflection process simple. Also, it would not be a good idea to start your resilience development program by implementing, let's say, 10 techniques at the same time. Most likely such a program will make you feel overwhelmed, and it will overlap negatively with your everyday schedule. You need to take it slowly, and in every coping goal you set, you need to consider the following general questions as you move forward:

- What was the goal?
- Where do I stand now and what steps did I do to reach here?

- How does my current state differ from my old state?
- What actions/amendments do I need to consider to improve my progress?
- What remains in order to reach my final destination?

Since in our everyday life we have a lot of things to take care of, we advise you to keep a log of your progress using a notebook that you will call the 'The Spartan W@rker Diary'. The purpose of being so precise when we reflect on our progress is to increase our motivation as we move forward. Every bit of progress will make you feel good about yourself, increasing your inner satisfaction and your willingness to go the extra mile towards your new self.

Let's start the fight!

In the following sections, we will present to you a variety of widely recognized behaviours that can help you to increase your levels of resilience, decrease your levels of stress and make you feel that you have the ultimate control of yourself – make you feel fierce and undefeatable like a Spartan!

Synchronize and develop your brain

We have already made a reference to Deepak Chopra's *Super Brain* and to our brain's unlimited capabilities. It would be a shame, when you are given the chance to drive a Lamborghini (your brain), to drive it like a bicycle. Eventually, though, the Lamborghini will think of itself as a bicycle if it never experiences its full capacity to run like the wind. You cannot know what you do not know. You cannot know what you have not experienced yet in life. Hence, we strongly suggest that a primary and important step of this process involves the development of your brain. You should trust us on that: the more you expand your general knowledge, the easier it will become to adjust yourself to difficult situations, thus avoiding the experience of unnecessary discomfort. Research supports that learning helps the brain remain active in older age, so if you embrace this approach, you will continue to maintain an active and fast-processing brain as you become older (Chopra & Tanzi, 2012). Through the learning process, our brain constantly assimilates incoming information, thus making learning and the development of new skills easier. Most importantly, though, we boost our self-esteem, since we feel more confident and we have a better insight of the constructs that surround our life. We believe that we can confront any situation as we have more access to available information from which we can retrieve better and more efficient coping strategies. Such development of the brain can increase both your adaptability and self-confidence skills in the resilience matrix, ensuring your wellbeing at work and in your personal life. Developing your brain can lead to both professional advancement, thus improving your lifestyle, status and financial freedom, and to the formulation of better social relationships and of higher-quality personal time. It seems that knowledge makes us better people both for society and most importantly for ourselves, because if you do not feel good about yourself, then obviously you will not feel good about anyone else or about any aspect of your life.

In order to do so, though, you must demonstrate an internal motive and interest in what is happening in your life. This does not mean that you have to learn everything in life, just the things that are relevant to you, to your lifestyle and to your work. Believe us, your schedule will be full of 'things to do'. Stimulating your brain keeps you motivated and makes you feel 'alive'. Knowledge increases our ability to do our jobs more effectively, but most importantly knowledge synchronizes our brain and promotes wellbeing. Adopting such an approach eventually will create feelings of calmness within you, thus enabling you to make better decisions in life and enriching your resilience skills along the way.

So, you must always be curious to experience new things; you must always diversify in what you learn in order to keep routine out of your way. Try to allocate time equally between what we call 'light' and 'heavy' learning. For instance, if you are a talented musician, you cannot spend all of your time learning music (heavy learning); this would probably lead to isolation from every other joy in life. You should allocate time equally to other social activities, hobbies, everyday common tasks etc. (light learning). There must be a balance between learning and acquiring new experiences and knowledge and personal life. Everything you do is linked to the development of a different and unique set of skills. The more the activities you undertake, the more you synchronize and develop your brain towards resilience. For instance, if you try to solve a Sudoku numeric puzzle, you will stimulate your thinking and your problem-solving ability. If you go hiking in nature, you will stimulate your body and your senses through the direct experience of nature. Nowadays, you can waste some time each week to solve brain quizzes that you can freely find on the Internet. Believe us, it is a good break, especially when you are at work and you want to reboot your concentration. Try it! It can really work as a stress reduction tool, and if you do any of these activities after work and before returning to your home life, it can work as a defusing agent for a more relaxed evening for you and your loved ones.

Another helpful behaviour is that of investing in your personal development. When we say personal development, we do not mean only the process of developing hard skills through university studies or learning a foreign language, although all of these constitute important assets upon which we build our careers. We also mean that you need to devote some time to developing a number of soft skills that can improve your communication with others, the ways through which you interact and create strong emotional ties with others or your spirituality. Also you could develop the creative/artistic side of yourself by learning how to play a new musical instrument, painting, modelling, dancing etc. Basically, every little thing that makes you feel good in your everyday life can also work as an excellent buffer against stress due to the fact that such activities can distract your attention from any work problems or obligations that you might have and make you connect with your inner self. Summing up, we want to give you a tip of advice: Since your time is scarce, try to allocate your energy and resources in the best possible combination between light and heavy learning. So recognize your needs/ wants and move on to the creation of your new self. Try to keep a balance in your choices by selecting some activities that are related to your work and some activities that are related to your inner self. Stretch your brain, stretch your body and be sure that you are heading in the correct direction, towards general wellbeing and satisfaction in life. Spartans were considered as the best warriors in ancient history, but at the same time they were good in sports and in activities such as dancing and singing, because they considered such activities as natural stimulants for their spirit. Their choice of lifestyle was responsible for the development and synchronization of their brain and also for their high resilience levels.

Become more positive

The experience of positive emotions makes us feel good. The most common positive emotions, according to Fredrickson (2009), are 'joy, gratitude, serenity, interest, hope, pride, amusement, inspiration, awe and love'. Keeping a balance between positive and negative emotions in life promotes life satisfaction and wellbeing (Diener & Larsen, 1993). Sometimes, life can be hard, but even in such times people can experience positive emotions through aiming to find a positive meaning in the hardship itself (Fredrickson, 2000). Whether a situation will be considered positive or negative to us depends on how we perceive the situation itself. By changing your mindset and becoming more positive, you will reduce the negativity in your life and you will live more fully. There is a give-and-take relationship between positive emotions and positive meaning (Fredrickson, 2000):

- Finding a positive meaning in any given situation precipitates the manifestation of positive emotions.
- The heightened experience of positive emotions in everyday life will increase the probability of experiencing positive meaning in future events.

In other words, positive emotions help us cope better with hardship, and the better we cope in life, the more positive emotions we will experience in the future. This cycle promotes the development of our resilience and the improvement of our psychological wellbeing.

We are surrounded by negativity wherever we go. During the turbulent and stressful times that we are living in, people have become more negative. They think negatively, and in turns they experience a number of negative emotions such as anger, fear and sadness. Most likely you experience the same negative emotions when you are feeling stressed and pressured by the demands of life.

Negative thoughts tend to disturb our everyday functions. When we start thinking negatively, it seems that negative thoughts start to multiply and thus increase our stress levels. Moreover, negative thinking seems to be contagious. Surely, you are aware of people who you consider as toxic and negative, and you try to avoid interacting with them when you meet them. By replacing our negative thoughts with more positive ones we promote our overall wellbeing. There are many techniques that one can use in order to release some tension, relax and send away any negative thinking and emotions (i.e. relaxation techniques, biofeedback, meditation and yoga). Here we present to you an exercise that you can use to make you feel more positive when dealing with adversity:

- Take a moment to reflect the situation and the effect that it has on you. What are the negative feelings that emerge? Is this the first time that you are dealing with such an adverse situation?
- Understand that adversities happen and that this will also happen in the future.
- It is the way that you perceive and handle the adversity that really matters.
- Acknowledge the presence of your thoughts and your emotions and accept them as they are. Do not try to change them.
- Analyze the situation, and instead of multiplying the negative experience through your thoughts, aim to find ways to overcome it. The faster you do that, the faster you will start shifting to positivism again.
- After dealing with the adverse situation, take a moment to think how it occurred. Process that in order to ensure that the same situation will not affect you in the future.
- Learn from the negative experience; see it as a challenge and as a route towards your more resilient self.

Invest in increasing your positive emotions in your everyday life and you will improve your mental strength, your physical health and the level of your resilience.

Take it slow

Nowadays, for the majority of the population, life seems to flow in a fast-forward pace. We are in a constant pursuit of something. What you need to realize, though, is that your to-do list will never end. Even if you manage to erase everything from your list today, the next day your to-do list will be full again. This is a reality that you need to accept. You need to take it slow. We know that just by saying to you: 'Do not rush', 'Do not overload yourself' or in general 'Try to take it easy in life' will not make things change instantly. The pressure at work and in your personal life and not being able to adapt to everyday demands are quite stressful by themselves. Hence, such recommendations that will not bring change instantly most probably will make you more worried, thus increasing your stress levels even more. Of course everything depends on personality: some individuals tend to rush more than others, and this is the most worrying part, since rushing does not necessarily constitute a problem when there is a real need. But what happens when rushing becomes a habit or a real way of life? Especially in the work domain, such rushing is characteristic of employees who are considered as effective, competitive and productive and who maintain a high work pace. Such employees, though, tend to be the ones who are rewarded with promotions and better pay and benefits, so it is difficult for them to understand the value of taking it slow, since taking it fast creates a sense of job security and is perceived through the organizational structure as a critical factor towards occupational success. Well, this is the reality of the modern work environment, a reality that produces several negative effects on your health due to the experienced stress that comes along with the adoption of such a lifestyle, especially when such a lifestyle becomes an inseparable part of your personal life. Taking it slow does not mean not doing anything; it rather means to organize your day better, to follow a more steady pace, to take breaks when you start feeling overloaded, to undertake activities that make you feel happy and relaxed, to have time for yourself and to understand that change needs time and requires slow but ongoing progress.

Ancient Spartans were usually taking it slow in their lives, and they were fierce and in an alarm stage only during battles and periods of crisis. They did not attempt to train themselves within a year to go to war. Both men and women were training for war for their whole life, men to be ready for fight and women to be strong in organizing whatever was needed during men's absence in Sparta. They had programmed their lives from early childhood to become what exactly they wanted to: highly resilient and stress-tolerant people. They were stress tolerant because they had faith in themselves and in their abilities, so they defied even death in battle, because they were well aware of the fact that they were trained better than anyone else in battle skills. This is the lifestyle of the Spartan W@rker.

The Spartan W@rker aims to adopt a lifestyle that will eventually distinguish him/her from other people. Although in the beginning taking it slow will make you feel strange, eventually it will save you from unnecessary arousal and discomfort because it will make you feel calm, and thus it will enable you to make better decisions in life.

If you consider yourself as a 'rushing' individual or if you just feel that you want to take it slow in life, you need to check your Type A behaviour pattern (individuals who are characterized by a fast-paced lifestyle, impatience, tenseness etc.). Take some time to run the following test (Table 7.1) to see whether you are more of a Type A or of a Type B person.

Table 7.1 Type A and B behaviours

Casual about time	1 2 3 4 5 6 7 8 9 10 11	Never late
Not competitive	1 2 3 4 5 6 7 8 9 10 11	Very competitive
Good listener	1 2 3 4 5 6 7 8 9 10 11	Anticipates what others are going to say (nods, interrupts, finishes for them)
Never feels rushed (even under pressure)	1 2 3 4 5 6 7 8 9 10 11	Always rushed
Can wait patiently	1 2 3 4 5 6 7 8 9 10 11	Impatient while waiting
Takes things one at a time	1 2 3 4 5 6 7 8 9 10 11	Tries to do many things at once; thinks what he is about to do next
Slow, deliberate talker	1 2 3 4 5 6 7 8 9 10 11	Emphatic in speech (may pound the desk)
Cares about satisfying self no matter what others may think	1 2 3 4 5 6 7 8 9 10 11	Wants good job recognized by others
Slow doing things	1 2 3 4 5 6 7 8 9 10 11	Fast (eating, walking, etc.)
Easy going	1 2 3 4 5 6 7 8 9 10 11	Hard driving (pushing yourself and others)
Expresses feelings	1 2 3 4 5 6 7 8 9 10 11	Hides feelings
Many outside interests	1 2 3 4 5 6 7 8 9 10 11	Few outside interests
Unambitious	1 2 3 4 5 6 7 8 9 10 11	Ambitious
Casual	1 2 3 4 5 6 7 8 9 10 11	Eager to get things done
Type B 14	84	154 Type A

Source: Cooper's Adaptation of the Bortner Type A Scale (Cooper, Cooper & Eaker, 1988).

An ideal score tends to be around 84 (from 64 to 104). A score above 84 means that you are a Type A person. Some characteristics of a Type A person are:

- Impatient
- Fast talking and eating
- Excessive multitasking
- Always in a rush (i.e. when driving)
- Time cautious
- Highly competitive
- Highly ambitious.

Does this remind you of yourself in everyday life? If the answer is yes, you need to take some action to lower your score below 84 in order to become more of a Type B person, hence a person who will be able to react to external stressors in a more calmed and relaxed way. If you are more of a Type B person, then it means that you are taking life slowly; but once again we do not want you to take life so slowly, because this is not healthy either, so we want you to be somewhere in the middle in terms of score in the test in Table 7.1. The more Type A behaviours you display, the more the probability that in your everyday interactions you will feel stressed, aroused, aggressive and impatient and you will experience more negative physiological symptoms. Of course, not all Type A behaviours are negative. It always depends on other personality factors whether a high score in one behaviour will trigger high levels of stress and frustration or not, according to the meaning that each of us ascribe to each situation (e.g. being highly ambitious may not pose a problem for you).

To conclude, in order to lower your Type A scores, you will have to work on your time management skills, to modify your internal urges and thinking patterns that trigger rushing behaviours in the first place. It would also be useful to experiment on relaxation techniques like meditation and breathing techniques (we will elaborate further in the following sections on these concepts). The more you remind yourself that you are a human being and not a human robot every time you experience any of the aforementioned symptoms, the more you will slow your pace and experience the benefits in your everyday life.

Foster your emotional intelligence (EI)

The role of emotions in an individual's work and personal life is of paramount importance when the concepts of stress reduction and resilience building are being examined. Most people are in a constant process to reduce the experience of emotional discomfort in their lives and to maintain an internal balance, a sense of equilibrium and homeostasis. Again, Spartan warriors appear to have understood this fact, and they had managed to arrive at such levels that enabled them to withstand a harsh upbringing and demanding situations in life, while at the same time they maintained their homeostasis and performance levels intact. We believe that such characteristics are included in the set of competencies that underlie the concept of emotional intelligence. Emotional intelligence reflects the abilities of an individual (i.e. emotional, personal and social) to recognize experienced emotions and to efficiently combine them into an interplay between thoughts and behaviours, with the aim to manage the demands and pressures of everyday life to a satisfactory extent (Bar-On, 1997). In accordance with this definition, one could easily argue that emotions also affect our thoughts and behaviours, and in moments of crisis, emotions are usually negative. In such instances, both at work and in personal life, the Spartan W@rker who has nurtured emotional intelligence remains more positive when compared to others who do not understand the role of emotions in our everyday life. In contrast with IQ, which is more stable throughout the lifespan of a person, emotional intelligence can be improved through training and learning. Even better, it has been found that individuals who demonstrated high levels of emotional intelligence also showed increased levels of overall wellbeing and work performance and decreased levels of stress (Slaski & Cartwright, 2002).

Daniel Goleman's (2000) model of EI that comprises four emotional and social competencies and highlights the effectiveness of our interactions with others both in work and personal settings. The four competencies are the following, and we discussed them in detail in Chapter 6:

1 Self-awareness
2 Self-management
3 Social awareness
4 Social skills

Moving forward, let's elaborate on some ways through which you can enhance your emotional intelligence. We will briefly present you four techniques that we consider valuable in order for you to start building upon your emotional intelligence capabilities. Start experimenting on these tools, and you will feel the benefits of being emotional intelligent in your everyday life. For more techniques, search the literature under Daniel Goleman (for example, Goleman, 1995; Boyatzis, Goleman & Rhee, 2000), who is one of the most influential thinkers on the topic of EI.

Active/genuine listening

Active/genuine listening will help you to become more self-aware and to improve your social skills, your emotional self-control and your feelings of empathy towards others. Basically, through the improvement of your listening skills you increase the possibilities of forming more meaningful and trustworthy relationships with others and of collecting all the necessary information that you will probably use in the face of a stressful situation. To succeed at that, you will need to evaluate your current attitudes towards the person in front of you, trying to be present when the person speaks, even when the topic is not of high interest to you. You must show respect to the speaker, treating him/her as an equal, and allocate your focus of attention towards him/her during the conversation. Everyone appreciates an audience that is actively listening and expands the discussion one step further. This condition creates feelings of warmth and proximity between the speaker and the listener, reflecting a strong relationship between them either at work or in personal life. Practicing this skill in everyday discussions will prepare you to behave similarly under stressful working conditions, showing to others that you are capable of handling any difficult situation or project with the same ease as you would have done during a social chat.

Expressing gratitude

Expressing gratitude is another way through which you can increase your self-awareness, self-management and social skills. The aim of expressing gratitude is to make you view life in a more positive way and to become grateful for what and whom you have around you (i.e. family, friends, colleagues). Keeping that in mind, even when everything around you looks like a mess, you should consider expressing gratitude to the people around you in your office and to those who are close to you. This action will generate in turn a positive energy and a cooperative reaction by others, and, especially in the work terrain, it will create a flow of energy that will positively affect goal completion and enhanced productivity. By expressing gratitude and being friendly to other human beings, you will compel them to lower their defences and come closer to you, because kindness exists within us and we are waiting to express it, but due to the modern way of life and the feelings of competition, we tend to be always on alert when interacting with others. Well, life can become simpler if you simply change your attitude towards others. Spartans were fond of the element of group cohesion and bonding and demonstrated that to those close to them, and they were committed and grateful towards Sparta in general. This was true until the end of their lives, and that is why they succeeded in fighting obstacles as one, and they did that very well indeed. So why not follow their lead? Just saying thanks to someone is a good way to express feelings of gratitude – it is so simple sometimes.

Think before you act

'Think before you act' is another technique that will help you to increase self-awareness, emotional self-control and the way you influence others. Every action you decide to take stimulates a response, and every individual might respond differently to the same action. This means that you should be very thoughtful about the emotional impact that your action will have on others even before you act. If you want to experience success in life, and especially in your job, you need to be quite conscious of what you are saying and when you are saying it. In moments of crisis you need to be a model of positive inspiration, and this needs to become your second nature. Always try to be fun, optimistic, kind and motivating towards others, because most of the time everyone just needs a little push to carry on. When the crisis is over, you can give constructive feedback regarding the things that annoyed you in the first place, without holding a critical stance but with empathy and motivation. If you want to be the best in whatever you do, you need to include these EI skills in your life, because through how you act and what you say is how other people tend to perceive you as a person. Think about it for a moment: do you want others to smile when they see you, or do you want them to avoid interacting with you?

Induce motive to yourself

'Induce motive to yourself' is another technique that will help you to increase your self-confidence and self-management skills in order to achieve your goals, and it will help you to strengthen your vision. We all possess strong qualities that, if we take advantage of them, will help us to succeed at both the personal and professional level. These are the qualities that we further need to explore and develop because through these qualities we achieve things, we feel better and more confident for ourselves and we become motivated in going the extra mile when needed. It is important to recognize your qualities so as to increase your motivation and strengthen your commitment towards your vision. Based on the Spartan W@rker philosophy, teamwork and social support are very important elements for success. You might have the best ideas and be highly motivated, but you cannot do everything alone. You put on the table all your strong qualities, but other people's qualities are needed, too, to complete the puzzle of success. So, as a Spartan, demonstrate your abilities with a positive mentality and high level of motivation. Your efforts and commitment will be recognized and appreciated by others, and people will try to connect with you even more. Remember that you need to motivate and inspire yourself first, and then others will be inspired through your deeds and philosophy in life.

The importance of emotional intelligence in difficult and strenuous times is very critical, since heightened levels of emotional arousal require high self-control, adaptability and a decisive response to be adequately managed. In fact, increased EI skills are needed to protect yourself and to comprehend other people who are involved in your everyday obligations, either at work and/or in your personal life, especially in situations where it is very difficult to escape and you need to keep going. Managing your emotions and your relationships with others is not an easy thing and requires a large volume of patience, persistence and acceptance of others. It is important to give ourselves the necessary time to develop EI skills through the trial and error process; if you do, you soon will experience the benefits that stem from exerting control on the most important factor that will help you succeed in life, which is nothing more than your inner self.

Social support

The concept of social support is very important in resilience literature and constitutes a significant element of the models (resilience, psychological hardiness, mental toughness, EI) presented so far in our quest to define what characteristics a true Spartan W@rker must possess. To succeed in work and in life in general, you need two elements: you and the others around you. You cannot succeed if you cannot control yourself, your emotions and your urges, but also you cannot succeed if you do not have the support of your colleagues during a difficult work project or the support of your family during turbulent times. Research about the effect of buffering hypothesis suggests that social support can work as a shield against the negative effects of stressful conditions and the impact of these conditions in the psychological wellbeing of the individual. This happens because social support assists in the modification of the primary appraisal of the stressor by reducing its impact, which in turns enables the individual to cope better with stress (LaRocco, House & French, 1980). So how do you build a strong social support network at work (of course the same techniques apply to your personal relationships too)? Here we present you some techniques that you can follow:

• Be loyal: If you want other people to be there when you need them, you have to show loyalty to them through your sayings and actions. Interact with your colleagues, and when your work schedule is not so heavy, try to offer some help to them during a demanding project. Explain to them that they can count on you if they ever need help. Believe us, this will alleviate some of the burden of their everyday work life just by knowing that there is someone willing to help them in times of crisis. By showing sincere loyalty, you will feel good about yourself, but most importantly you will have some people to count on when you will come to deal with similar situations.

- Be present both in times of success and in times of failure: Working life has its ups and downs. One day we are cheering up due to the successful completion of a project, and the next day something can go wrong that negatively affects the psychology of the team. You should act as an exemplar in both cases. First, when you achieve a goal, share the victory with the others around you and do not take the credit only for yourself; otherwise, nobody will be there to support you when a possible failure occurs. Involve others in your work and thank them for their contribution when successfully completing a project. Send an email to the entire office informing them of the positive outcome and also mention the names of the colleagues who helped you. Through this you will create strong bonds and increase group cohesion. In the same vein, when a failure knocks on the door, do not run to hide behind your colleagues' backs; it is preferable to stay in front and take responsibility for your actions. This will be much appreciated by everyone and will also work positively for your business ethos. Moreover, when one of your colleagues confronts failure, you should not use negative criticism, but you should try to propose solutions that will help overcome the negative situation. Try to be present for both good and bad days at work and you will create a strong social support network.

- Show you care: We believe that colleagues are not just colleagues, they are human beings, so be empathetic toward the problems they might encounter both at work and in their personal lives. At the end of the day, if an individual is feeling stressed, this will negatively affect the individual's levels of performance and overall wellbeing, which in turn will negatively affect the effectiveness of the whole organization. When you feel that this is the case, proactively offer your help. Become a natural helper and become a positive figure in your work environment. As discussed previously, in the EI section, you should actively listen to your colleagues' concerns and try to help them to reduce their tension. If the problem is work-related, try to arrange a meeting to discuss how this can be dealt. If the problem consists of personal matters, make the necessary arrangements to offer to the individual some flexibility to leave the office earlier in order to resolve the issue as soon as possible. If you have the authority, do it by yourself; otherwise, ask permission from the management. This will restore work–life balance to the individual, which at the same time will increase team bonding and enrich your social support network.

Start working on these techniques and you will start experiencing the benefits of social support by becoming more resilient and less susceptible to stress.

Inject some humour into your life

Humour has been found to work as a buffer against stress. The American Psychiatric Association (APA, 2000), has described humour as a successful coping skill that has been found to increase life satisfaction and to promote homeostasis and a sense of internal balance. Humour during difficult situations was found to shift the focus of attention away from the stressor, thus decreasing individuals' experienced levels of stress (Abel, 2002). A Spartan W@rker, even if he/she takes life events seriously, does not become overwhelmed by the obstacles and prefers to make 'fun' of the negative situations, since it is considered much healthier not to worry about things that cannot change (because they have already occurred) instead of being constantly anxious. According to Lazarus and Folkman (1984), there is a relationship between humour and stress, with humour working as a pleasant distraction that shifts away the focus of attention from the potential threat. Through the use of humour, you can keep negative arousal levels low, and you can also gain precious time when you are in the stress arena by better evaluating the situation and proceeding with the most efficient problem-focused strategy (Straub, 2002).

Hence, we suggest that you should always try to keep this characteristic present in your everyday life. You should always try to find the beauty in every situation. Whether you experience a negative event alone or within a team, you should use humour as an initial attempt to deal with stress. Use humour when you are dealing with a problem at work with your colleagues, and you will see the positive contagious effect that you will have on others. During a crisis, people tend to listen and to attach themselves to the ones who seem to cope better, and the Spartan W@rker always tries to overcome the difficulties, no matter what.

Laughter is a key element of humour. It seems that one cannot do one without the other, so put a smile on your face, since laughter can help you reduce feelings of stress and anxiety. Do not just wait for something funny to happen: take the initiative and create a joyful moment for you and the others around you. Be the charming and humoristic individual who others would like to be with. Either tell a joke or share a funny story, but most importantly aim to find the funny side of a stressful and demanding situation; it will just make things lighter and easier to handle. Try to keep a log (using your Spartan W@rker Diary) of a minimum of two moments in your day where you laughed and you injected some humour into your life. Increase such moments in your everyday life, and simultaneously you will see your general wellbeing and productivity levels increase, too.

Be physically active

The Spartan warriors gave extra weight to their physical condition. They respected their body, since they believed that a strong body could aid them to surpass every obstacle met along their way. The Spartan W@rker understands that the body should be treated like a piece of ancient Greek marble. In the beginning a marble is shapeless, but as you sculpture it, it slowly takes form and it becomes a precious artefact – and this is how you should view your body, like the most precious possession of your life. A well-known saying of the ancient world was *nous igiis en somati igii*, which implied that a healthy mind exists within a healthy body.

The benefits of exercise on health and stress tolerance are well documented in the scientific literature for many decades now (Van Doornen & De Geus, 1989; Nieman, 1998). However, people tend to forget that as they rush throughout the day trying to catch up with all their obligations. 'I do not have time' is one of the most common excuses that one usually hears. Physical exercise should not be seen as part of your everyday routine or a nice-to-have activity, if you can afford some time within your compact schedule. Unfortunately, it does not work this way, and the benefits of exercise require some time to become apparent as in the case of the marble when the artist starts working on it. But the benefits are far too important to ignore them. Physical exercise works as a protective mechanism against physical illnesses, such as heart disease, obesity, musculoskeletal problems and so on. Likewise, physical exercise can reduce stress levels and anxiety, and it can also alleviate depressive symptoms. It is important to understand that physical exercise does not necessarily mean that you have to dedicate three hours per day at the gym in order to remain healthy. Everything centres around your general lifestyle, a fact that is also supported by research, which states that healthy middle-aged individuals who jog, swim, climb stairs, do gardening and spend time in physically intense leisure activities exhibit better overall wellbeing and less mortality risks (Yu, Yarnell, Sweetnam & Murray, 2003). It does not matter which kind of exercise you usually prefer to do or with what intensity; it is important to know that even short periods of daily exercise can produce multiple benefits for you.

It is up to you to decide the type of exercise you would like to do. The options are countless, and they can be either a sport or a hobby or even household work that requires some physical activity and muscular effort (e.g. gardening). If you want to become a Spartan W@rker, you must include physical exercise in your life to experience the following benefits:

- Better overall health
- Increased strength and flexibility
- Reduced levels of stress and anxiety
- Stronger immune system
- Better weight control and better body posture
- Feelings of relaxation and calmness
- Higher levels of energy and stamina
- Better quality of sleep
- Improved cognitive function and memory
- Feelings of happiness and positive mood
- Higher self-esteem and self-confidence
- Decreased feelings of sadness.

The benefits of exercise are many, and if you want to succeed both in your professional and personal life, you need to include physical exercise in your lifestyle. A Spartan W@rker understands that exercise fosters overall well-being, maintains internal balance and improves concentration, since it is an activity that does not allow negative multitasking (being occupied with a number of tasks at the same time, resulting in underperformance). You have to be focused on what you do in order to perform the exercise well and avoid injury. Fortunately, improved concentration is also transferred into your working life, thus helping you to avoid negative multitasking. Therefore, you can be concentrated for many hours and you will see your productivity rising to the sky. Moreover, exercise boosts your self-esteem. Every positive change in your body (remember the piece of marble mentioned before), such as weight loss or increase of strength and stamina, will boost you up and will make you feel more self-confident. With higher self-esteem and self-confidence comes higher resilience and thus stress reduction in all aspects of life.

As you read these paragraphs, most probably you are thinking of your current exercise status. You might exercise a lot, moderately or not at all. When it comes to exercise, the most important factor is, as we mentioned previously, to include it in your lifestyle and also to avoid boredom as you move forward. There are many alternatives from which you can choose when it comes to exercise. You might already perform some of them which you do not consider as activities that can be tagged as exercise; however, they are truly beneficial.

Hence, let's start with some easy and less demanding everyday activities. You should try to perform some of the following activities on a daily basis:

- Use your bicycle to go to work or to any other appointment.
- Try to walk as much as possible for your everyday shopping and even when you are in the office. Do not send an email; walk to your colleague's office and discuss in person. It will also strengthen work relationships.
- Instead of the elevator, use the stairs.
- Dedicate some time for the household chores.
- In the morning or after work, go for a walk alone, with company or with your pet.

Believe us when we say so: these activities will keep your tension levels low throughout the work day and will diffuse some pressure. This will save you from the experience of unnecessary discomfort and will make you pass the rest of the day nicely.

Moving forward, in order to incorporate a proper exercise schedule, you should try to include some of the following aerobic and recreational activities for at least 20–30 minutes three to five times per week:

- Running
- Swimming
- Biking
- Hiking
- Sports (i.e. basketball, volleyball, tennis, golf, football).

Finally, two to three times per week you should try to include some of the following stretching and strengthening activities:

- Weight lifting
- Push-ups/pull-ups
- Martial arts
- Yoga
- Pilates
- Dancing
- Stretching.

All that might seem too much for you, but they are not – you just need to incorporate this plan into your current activity schedule. If you do not exercise at all, then you need to start slowly by increasing your everyday activities, such as walking, using the stairs etc. This will activate your muscles and nerves of your body, and you will start experiencing some of the benefits that exercise can offer. Try to increase the duration of such activities in your everyday life, and when you feel confident enough, then decide which form of exercise or recreational activity is more appropriate for you and include it in your schedule.

If you are generally active, then you can enrich your schedule and combine many forms of exercise to get the most out of it. Plan your activities with the aim of keeping a balance between aerobic, strength and stretching exercises. For instance, you could do three trainings per week where you can combine running, weight lifting and push-ups/pull-ups together. In addition, you can add in your schedule some yoga, Pilates or stretching lessons one or two times per week. If at some point you feel bored, then try to interchange the activities as an attempt to break the routine. It will be helpful for you to plan your daily schedule of exercise the night before, after having taken into account the rest of your obligations. For instance, some people prefer to exercise early in the morning before going to work or beginning their day because it helps them to cope better throughout the day, while others prefer to exercise late in the afternoon. It is up to you how you will plan your exercise schedule; the first step is to plan it, and even if you do not feel good about it, to pass through the door of the gym. Always remember that in order to be fit, you should 'fit' exercise in your demanding schedule, no matter what. Do not let excuses and pretexts stop you. We understand that time is precious, but you should also understand that your wellbeing is also far more precious. Try to restrict the time you spent in front of a screen. Have you ever calculated your daily screen time, that is the time you spent watching TV, using your laptop, or surfing the Internet with your smart phone? You will be amazed of the amount of time spent in total. Reduce this time to half and you will probably gain the time needed to exercise.

To conclude, it is simple as that. The more time you invest in exercise, the more dynamic, full of energy and stress tolerant you will become in your everyday life, making you more productive at work and a better and happier person in your private life.

Adopt a healthy lifestyle

What is your opinion about your lifestyle? Do you perceive yourself as someone who follows a number of healthy habits in everyday life? Have you ever thought about it, and do you see any importance in cultivating a healthy lifestyle?

Well, if you haven't already thought about it, and if you want to become a resilient Spartan W@rker in life, you should start considering it. Exercise, nutrition, obesity, smoking, alcohol consumption, screen time and sleep are factors that either expand your available resources through which you manage to deal effectively with everyday hassles and obligations or absorb your energy and motivation, thus making you feel tired, unproductive and in a bad mood.

Take a minute to read this story:

Tom is a 32-year-old individual who works in a technology company. When he was younger he used to be a sportive guy as well as a person full of life. He used to hang around with friends, to care about his appearance and to criticize his friends because they were smoking and eating 'junk' food regularly. Everything seemed perfect, but the only thing that he could not cope well with was the time spent playing video games and in front of the TV. He could stay in front of a screen for hours, losing perception of time, but since all other things were running smoothly, he did not care too much.

When he finished school and began university studies, life became harsher for him. He became stressed about the courses and the exams, and he preferred to stay home to study for prolonged periods. This was a wise decision characterizing a mature student. The problem was that at the same time he did not restrict screen time, so instead of continuing his social life after studying he preferred playing video games, because, as he said, video games have helped him dealing with stress. By behaving in such a way, he stopped himself from doing sports, going out with friends and cooking healthy meals. Gradually, as the stress was accumulating, he started smoking and drinking alcohol. During the weekends, he was going out and consuming large quantities of alcohol, claiming that alcohol was making him relax and forget the harsh student life. Finally, his sleeping patterns were becoming unstable because he preferred staying wake until late watching movies either alone or with friends. He perceived the situation to be a typical one of a student life, and he was trying to convince himself that he will change his lifestyle again as soon as he completed his studies.

At 32, Tom keeps on with the same lifestyle. He has become even more isolated, having only a couple of friends with whom he shares the same interests. You can imagine him waking up tired in the morning, since he does not sleep more than four hours and consumes alcohol on a regular basis. He spends his working day in front of a screen, and he continues to do so when he returns home. He does not eat a proper breakfast, smokes a pack of cigarettes per day and at night still orders 'junk' food. There is no physical exercise or physical activity in his everyday life. Tom understands his condition, but now he thinks that there is no way out.

We agree that change does not come easily, especially when you have learned to follow a specific lifestyle for years. In order for change to come you must first comprehend the benefits of a healthy lifestyle. Then you should start gradually and regularly to implement changes in your everyday schedule and habits. You cannot do everything at once, so you will need to set your priorities. For instance, if you want to start exercising but you have some extra weight that makes exercise difficult, you should focus first on losing some weight through proper nutrition and then try to gradually insert some mild exercise in your schedule. Remember that you should always proceed by setting SMART goals. Ancient Spartans did not become the elite warriors of the ancient world within a night; they were training themselves both physically and mentally for years, but that was something normal for them since they knew that this was the only way to achieve perfection in life.

Here are some advices that will improve your lifestyle, covering a number of topics:

Nutrition

- To begin your day, consume a healthy breakfast that contains lean proteins and carbs. You can eat or drink dairy products, oats, honey, fresh juices, green tea etc., foods that will wake you up and help you to keep your energy throughout the day.
- Avoid grabbing snacks at work; most probably they will be unhealthy. Ideally, bring with you some fruits, nuts and yogurt or toast and a light meal for lunch time. If for any reason you do not have time to prepare anything like that at home, either make a stop at the nearest food market in your way to work or during lunch break or try to locate the healthy options in the food catalogue when you order food at work.
- After work try to consume a healthy dinner with salad and add some protein.
- Avoid excess consumption of fats throughout the day. Try to choose meals that include low-fat, low-cholesterol, low-sodium and high-fibre items.
- Throughout the day, avoid dehydrating. Do not force yourself to drink gallons of water per day; you should rather drink when you feel thirsty. Water is imperative for all the functions of your body and also for your brain functions.
- Avoid drinking many coffees throughout the day; eventually they will not give you an extra boost but will rather make you nervous. Instead drink tea, which is more beneficial for your health and also helps you concentrate during difficult times.
- During weekends you can give a 'free day' to yourself regarding the things that you can eat. Do not exaggerate, but reward yourself for the demanding week you have passed.

- Avoid consuming too much alcohol. A glass of red wine or a glass of beer in the afternoon is more than enough, and you will experience the relaxation effects that alcohol can provide, defusing you after a demanding work day.
- Remember you are what you eat. Food gives you energy to make it through the day. If you consume junk food, your available resources will become depleted quickly enough, but if you eat healthy you will have fuel to run through the day, and you will even wake up the next day feeling lighter and more energetic.
- Follow such a nutrition schedule and you will lose the extra weight that you wish, but you will also become more physically and mentally healthy and you will strengthen your immune system against illness.

The benefits of a healthy diet are many, but we advise you to not overdo with it. All of us know someone who became miserable and unhappy due to obsessions underlying issues of nutrition. Wellbeing is something good, but as with everything in life we need to proceed with moderation. As the Greek philosophers were saying *pan metron ariston*, which means everything in moderation.

Smoking

Smoking has been linked to the manifestation of a number of negative con-sequences for health (heart disease, cancer etc.). The same stands for stress too, which according to the Health and Safety Executive (HSE, 2001) causes a number of health problems including cancer, cardiovascular diseases, gas-trointestinal problems and depression and leads to the adoption of a number of unhealthy habits such as smoking, alcohol consumption and drug use, which in turn can precipitate the manifestation of ill health. The relationship between smoking and stress is obvious, and you can understand how smok-ing can drain your energy levels and diminish your physical condition. The demanding schedule that you have in your everyday life does not allow you to waste any physical energy nor to undermine your health with a habit that at the end of the day does not offer you anything more than difficulty breathing.

At the same time, we understand that to quit smoking is not an easy task, since smoking is considered an addiction. You also should be informed that aside from the unhealthy tar and nicotine that can be found in cigarettes, one can also trace approximately 2,000 different chemical substances. For these reasons, if you are a regular smoker, we advise you to start making efforts to reduce smoking and eventually to stop it, since such a lifestyle change will enhance your overall health and energy levels and eventually will increase your performance in every aspect of your life.

Most probably, when you will start making your effort, your internal saboteur will emerge with some of the following assumptions:

- I cannot stop smoking; it is very difficult.
- I am very stressed in this period of my life, and smoking helps me to relax.
- I have heard that when you stop smoking, you put on weight.
- I have not smoked for two days and I do not feel well. I cannot tolerate this anymore; it makes me aggressive.

It is natural for such thoughts to arise, as usually happens with every change that you wish to accomplish in your lifestyle, but you should try to modify your thoughts by answering to yourself something like the following:

- It will be difficult to quit smoking in the beginning, but my future self will thank me when I will feel the beneficial changes in me.
- I am sure that I can find healthier ways to relax and substitute them for smoking.
- Gaining weight when quitting smoking does not happen to everyone, especially if I follow a healthy nutrition plan and do some form of physical exercise.
- I understand that the first two to three days will be quite difficult for me, both in my work and personal life, but I will inform the people who are close to me to be supportive in spite of my unstable mood during this period.

Some recommendations to help you quit smoking involve a visit to a physician, who would inform you regarding the available therapies in the market, to join stop-smoking groups and to work with a CBT therapist. Another popular trend for smoking cessation is nicotine patches/gums and electronic cigarettes, which can substitute for cigarette smoking and gradually reduce nicotine intake. Unfortunately, such nicotine replacement products have not escaped criticism due to the possible side effects that they might have.

In your effort to quit smoking, it is helpful to know that cigarette consumption is decreasing constantly for the majority of the population both in Europe and in the United States. If you are determined and you work on the modification of behaviours that are linked to smoking, you will definitely succeed, and you will soon enjoy a healthier and more productive life.

Sleep

Good sleep quality is considered vital for our everyday functions. Unfortunately, many people complain that they cannot sleep well or that they cannot sleep enough in order to restore their energy levels. Once again, stress seems to play a significant role in individuals' sleeping patterns. High levels of stress can precipitate the manifestation of a number of negative physiological symptoms, such as sleep loss, stomach problems and high blood pressure (Costa, 2003; Misra & Stokols, 2012). Subsequently, sleep problems/deprivation have been linked to the deterioration of both physical and psychological abilities and also to a decrease in performance (Moran, Eliyahu, Berlin, Hadad & Heled, 2007; Ford, Cerasoli, Higgins & Decesare, 2011).

All of this seems very disturbing, especially nowadays, when we hear that many people, due to the stress experienced at work, meet several sleep problems. People tell us that it is really difficult for them to switch themselves off from all their daily hassles before bedtime, which has as a result the experience of feelings of fatigue and insomnia,[1] and even if they manage to sleep, they wake up early feeling tired. It is well known that the human brain, without substantial sleep, is unable to preserve its biochemical and electrical balance, thus deteriorating the effectiveness of its functions and the capability of an individual to cope well with demanding situations (Quick, Quick, Nelson & Hurrell, 1997).

We all have specific and unique sleeping patterns which, when they become disturbed, produce discomfort for us, since sleep is considered the best way to rest and reboot our organism. Very important functions of the body are closely related to sleep, such as body temperature, hormonal secretion and metabolism. Generally, sleep replenishes your resources in order for you to be full-on for the activities of your next day, and based on latest research, sleep seems to reset overstimulated neuron synapses after a day of extensive neural activity (Miller, 2009). In order to become a Spartan W@rker, you must fully understand the value of sleep and the benefits that come along with that, since sleep will help you remain productive and full of energy throughout the day, both at work and in your personal/family life. Here we present some ways through which you can improve your sleeping patterns:

- Try to sleep regularly seven to eight hours every day, and you will soon experience a reduction of your stress levels.
- When you go to sleep, try to minimize light and noise exposure, especially in the morning hours, in order to avoid waking up early.
- Set your mobile phone to silence mode, since an email, a message, a notification or a call can disturb your sleep for good.
- If for any reason you have not managed to sleep well the previous night, try to replenish your sleeping time by taking 30- or even 15-minute naps during the day, since napping is considered useful in reducing feelings of sleepiness and in increasing performance levels.

- If you have to work until late in the afternoon, make sure that you will have finished at least an hour before going to bed, and try to do something that will calm you down and make you sleep easier.
- If you face sleep problems, try to do a relaxation exercise (you will find an example in the section 'Become mindful' later in this chapter), take a warm bath to release any tension or take a walk around your neighbourhood alone or with your pet.
- Avoid overeating or doing intense exercise during the night hours.
- Do not watch TV for a half an hour before you go to sleep, and definitely keep the TV switched off when you sleep, because the noise will prevent you from reaching deep levels of sleep.
- Even better, read a book for your enjoyment and you will fall asleep naturally.
- Try to maintain a consistent schedule of sleeping time. It will help you to sleep easier and also to wake up easier in the morning.
- If you are sensitive to caffeine, you should consider reducing caffeine intake.
- Consider the investment of a good mattress and pillow, since it will benefit you with a more comfortable and better quality sleep.
- If you cannot stop thinking about your next day's obligations, write a to-do list, since prioritizing and scheduling them will calm you down.

Every time that you are thinking why sleep is so important for your resilience, wellbeing and growth in life, remind yourself of the following:

- Sleep improves your memory and your productivity.
- Sleep boosts your immune system and keeps you healthy.
- Sleep helps you in maintaining a stable mood and enhances your psychological wellbeing.
- Sleeps improves your physical performance.
- Sleeps improves your creativity and sharpens your concentration.
- Sleep reduces your levels of stress throughout the day.

Become mindful

In recent years, a concept that has become quite popular, due to the benefits offered on both physical and psychological wellbeing, is mindfulness. Jon Kabat-Zinn (2012, p. 1) defines mindfulness as 'The awareness cultivated by paying attention on purpose, in the present moment, and nonjudgmentally to the unfolding of experience moment by moment'. According to Kabat-Zinn, mindfulness is the art of being conscious and aware of both internal and external experiences that occur in the present moment. Nothing else is more important, neither the past nor the future. Genuine experience of life is happening in the present moment, and for this reason you must seize every single moment and live it fully. Mindfulness is about experiencing your senses, like your breathing and the sensations of your body, in an effort to use them as an anchor to the present moment. This can be achieved through the use of Mindfulness-Based Stress Reduction (MBSR) programs that were firstly implemented by Kabat-Zinn at the Medical Center of the University of Massachusetts in 1979. MBSR programs comprise a mixture of techniques, such as mindfulness meditation, mindful eating, body awareness, relaxation techniques, breathing techniques and yoga, with the aim of making people more mindful, more resilient to uncontrollable change and less susceptible to stress. Recent research has supported the effectiveness of MBSR programs, with results demonstrating that MBSR significantly reduces stress levels and emotional exhaustion and improves feelings of positivism and overall quality of life (Nyklicek & Kuijpers, 2008).

You do not have to participate in any MBSR program in order to benefit from mindfulness. You can alternatively choose one, some or all of the techniques mentioned here and incorporate them in your everyday life to help you cope with stress and build up your resilience. The good thing with the majority of the techniques presented in this chapter is that they do not only help you to relax when you feel stressed, but if you practice some of them regularly they can work proactively, thus reducing experienced levels of stress in the first place.

We believe that when it comes to stress: 'Prevention is better than cure.' This is the philosophy of the Spartan W@rker: to do what is necessary to transform into a new and highly resilient self, where everything in life is being handled in a more efficient and effective way, regardless of the nature of the situation. Let's present to you the benefits of some of the mindfulness techniques. We will begin with a relaxation exercise, so afford some minutes to relax before you keep on reading further.

Relaxation exercise

Stress comes and goes in numerous ways throughout the day. Sometimes stress is good and makes us productive and fully engaged in what we do, and sometimes stress is bad and deteriorates our performance, creating anxiety and discomfort for us. But it is OK, and there is no need to panic, because as we have seen so far you have an extensive armoury in your hands that can help you manage stress and improve your resilience. There are numerous techniques that can alleviate stress, and one of them is called relaxation. Have you ever tried this approach against stress? If not, it is a very good and quick way to defuse the tension accumulated throughout the day or 'shut down' from everything that preoccupies you before going to sleep.

A brief relaxation exercise will require about 10 minutes of your time, but it will really relax you by lowering stress and tension in your mind and body. It will also restore your energy levels and make you feel more alive. Next we give you an example of a relaxation exercise that you can practice at home or at the office, preferably in a quiet place. Give it a try; it will only require a few minutes of your time:

- Try to make yourself comfortable by sitting in an upright or reclining position.
- Close your eyes slowly and bring your attention inwards.
- Start thinking of a place that you have been before that generates feelings of safety and serenity for you (a familiar environment like a beach, a mountain landscape, a small cafe that you like going to on weekends). If you cannot recall such a place, it's OK; just try to imagine a place that you would like to be that would be perfect for physical and mental relaxation. A place that is quiet, beautiful and stress free. . . .
- Stay in this place for a moment and start observing every little detail of it. How is the weather, is it day or night, is the place isolated or are there people, birds or any animals around you? Use every detail that you can while imagining the place.
- In this moment, try to picture yourself as being part of the environment, part of the relaxation image in your brain. Imagine experiencing the place by activating all your senses. See every detail, hear every sound, from the most intense to the most unnoticed ones that are coming from the background of the place. Smell all the scents and touch everything that exists in the grasp of your hands around you.
- Just be there in your comforting position and immensely enjoy this beautiful and relaxing environment that you have brought yourself into.
- As you deepen yourself in your thoughts and imagination, try to feel the calmness and peacefulness of the scenery and experience your body feeling lighter and more relaxed. Try to stay in this condition as much as you can.
- If during the relaxation process your mind drifts away back to the situation that made you feeling stressed in the first place or just travels somewhere else, it's OK. Do not be upset or critical of yourself; it is a normal function of your brain, and through practice such interruptions will become less and less, enhancing the overall sense of your relaxation. Just bring your attention and thoughts inwards again to the place of relaxation.

- After 7–10 minutes, open your eyes slowly and gently stretch your body, while at the same time you experience a calming sensation and a smile is being formed on your face.
- You can return to this place whenever you wish, so this place is there for you, and this exercise can make you experience peace and tranquillity in your mind and body.

Yoga

Yoga has become a popular way of exercise that combines both physical and psychological benefits for the individual. What is also very important when we talk about yoga is that it is considered one of the few exercises that, due to the postures it includes, exercises and detoxes the internal organs of the body. In a review of studies of yoga, researchers concluded that, among other things, yoga is very effective against stress, sleep disturbance and fatigue and that yoga contributes to a decrease in cholesterol levels and to an increase in flexibility and balance (Ross & Thomas, 2010). For all these reasons, we recommend that you make an effort to participate in a yoga lesson. To motivate you even more, here we present a list with some of yoga's benefits. Yoga practice:

- Improves your flexibility, through stretching your muscles when entering yoga poses
- Improves your respiratory system
- Leads to better weight control through balancing your metabolism
- Protects your body from physical injuries, since you become more flexible
- Supports your cardiovascular health
- Increases the strength of your muscles
- Improves your overall body posture
- Lowers your stress levels
- Improves your brain function and concentration
- Reduces chronic neck and back pain
- Can have positive effects against depression.

In addition, yoga provides you with a sense of calmness and stability that you can bring with you to your work environment and enable you to work focused for prolonged periods, thus increasing your productivity levels. Give it a chance and you will be amazed by the positive effect that it will have in your life. Today, one can take yoga lessons in almost every gym.

Meditation

Nowadays, meditation is considered a very popular technique that promotes psychological wellbeing. Experts suggest that companies should encourage their members to exercise meditation and yoga, since both have been found to have a positive contribution against stress (Cooper, Quick & Schabracq, 2015). Moreover, meditation has been found to alleviate some discomfort in cases of chronic pain (Kabat-Zinn, Lipworth & Bruney, 1985), to decrease the possibilities of heart disease (King & D'Cruz, 2002) and also to reduce symptoms of anxiety (Kabat-Zinn, Massion, Kristeller, Peterson, Fletcher, Pbert, Lenderking & Santorelli, 1992).

The benefits of mindfulness meditation are several, and we advise you to consider adding meditation to your everyday life. You can start slowly if you are inexperienced, exercising for 5–10 minutes in order to become familiar with the process. In the beginning, it might be convenient to start with some audio-guided meditation where you can hear soft white-noise music and some instructions for a number of exercises that include, among others, breathing techniques (we discuss and present an example here), relaxation techniques and body scan exercises. Through mindfulness meditation, you can increase your level of self-regulation, which helps you guide your attention consciously from moment to moment and consequently enables you to manage everyday obligations with a sense of engagement without being distracted by what is happening around you. Find here a short exercise as an example of how you can practice meditation:

- Wherever you are, try to locate an isolated and peaceful environment in which you can easily practice the exercise.
- As a suggestion, keep in mind that it is better to meditate with an empty stomach.
- Take a comfortable position and lie down. If feasible, remove your shoes or even wear something comfy.
- Do not cross your arms and legs, and put both hands on your stomach in order to regulate your breathing rate.
- Start breathing slowly and bring your attention inwards.
- You may soften your gaze or close your eyes; both are perfectly fine.
- If your thoughts are travelling around or if you become distracted due to uncontrollable environmental factors, avoid being judgmental. Be aware of their existence and constantly try to return your attention inwards.
- As you breathe, start shifting your attention towards each part of your body, starting from the head and moving down to your shoulders, chest, torso and legs. Notice any tension or sensation arising from your body while breathing normally.
- After finishing this body scan exercise, continue breathing slowly.

- During meditation, it is also very beneficial to repeat a short phrase, a mantra, at the time you exhale. For instance, you can repeat 'I am strong' or 'I am calm' or 'I am happy'. The options are unlimited, so use the phrase that represents you better.
- Whenever you want, you can stop doing the exercise. There are no time limits; it is up to you.

Try to meditate regularly, and you will soon experience serenity and calmness in your everyday busy life. Trust us on that. Needless to say, the benefits of meditation underlying work productivity and performance are massive. Your work days will be calmer and more relaxed than they used to be, which will help you focus only on the important things. Here you can read some of the benefits that mindfulness meditation has to offer:

- Reduces feelings of stress, anxiety, anger and depression
- Creates more appreciation of life
- Boosts the immune system
- Enables better sleep quality
- Improves brain function
- Supports inner balance and calmness
- Helps in thought regulation
- Increases your energy levels.

Breathing techniques

Breathing is the most important function of our body. Without breath there is no life. The rhythm of your breath reveals the state of your body, whether you experience tension or not. In stressful situations where you experience tension, your breath is short, rapid and unstable, and you tend to breathe through your chest only. In contrast, when you are calm, your breath is stable, with a good pace, and you tend to breathe deeply from your abdomen area.

When breathing only through your chest, your lungs do not operate fully, and hence less oxygen enters into the bloodstream, which as a consequence distributes fewer nutrients to the tissues. Training yourself to breathe through the abdomen can help you to alleviate some physical symptoms of stress, and as you practice it and become more experienced, you can even reach a relaxation state whenever you want. Try the following exercise, which will help you reduce any signs of tension through the use of abdominal breathing, and note the effect that it had on you:

1 To begin the exercise, take a comfortable position in a quiet and relaxing place of your preference.
2 Put one of your hands on your abdomen, located exactly below your rib cage, and the other on your chest.

3   When you feel comfortable in your position, inhale slowly but deeply from your nose and not from your mouth, trying to expand only your abdomen area and not your chest. Use both your hands to regulate breathing in this way.

4   After taking a full breath, pause for a moment, and then completely exhale fully with a steady and controllable pace, either from your nose or mouth; both ways are absolutely fine.

5   In the beginning, the exercise might seem quite demanding to you, so it would be a good idea to count in each breath cycle. Breathe in for four seconds, hold your breath for one second and then exhale slowly for another four seconds. In each exhalation, focus to release some tension from your body.

Aim to practice this form of abdominal breathing 4–5 minutes daily for the next two weeks, and you will start gradually experiencing its benefits. Abdominal breathing positively affects your autonomic nervous system, which is responsible for the control of all the autonomous functions of the human body, such as breathing, heart rate and digestion.

Especially during work, you should be aware of your breathing. When we have an important meeting, we tend to move quickly and to increase our breathing rate. This means that we are entering the stress arena. The Spartan W@rker, understands what happens to the organism and consciously slows down his/her movements and breathes deeply to defuse some tension before entering into the meeting room. The Spartan W@rker is confident about his/her abilities and also is quite flexible in adjusting to difficult situations at work and in personal life. Practice and preparation for such stressful moments is the key to success.

Summary

In this chapter, we presented a number of ways through which you can change your mindset and lifestyle and become more tolerant of stress. We gave several examples with detailed instructions, and we proposed some ways through which you can adjust your everyday life to implement some of the coping techniques and to manage your time effectively. Some of the techniques are directly aimed at building resilience and defusing stress symptoms, while others have a more indirect impact on resilience and stress. We also understand that we have presented to you a lot of material, so in the next chapter we will present to you a six-day plan incorporating a number of activities that will help you get started. We have named that the Spartan 6-day Bootcamp!

Note

1 Insomnia is a subjective problem of insufficient or nonrestorative sleep despite an adequate opportunity to sleep' (Gillin & Byerley, 1990).

References

Abel, M. H. (2002). Humor, Stress and Coping Strategies. *Humor-International Journal of Humor Research*, 15, 365–381.

American Psychiatric Association. (2000). *Diagnostic and Statistical Manual of Mental Disorders*. 4th ed. Washington, DC: Author.

Bar-On, R. (1997). *EQi: Bar-On Emotional Quotient Inventory*. Toronto: Multi-Health Systems.

Boyatzis, R. E., Goleman, D., & Rhee, K. (2000). Clustering Competence in Emotional In- Telligence: Insights From the Emotional Competence Inventory (ECI). In R. Bar-On & J. D. A. Parker (Eds.), *The Handbook of Emotional Intelligence: Theory, Development, Assessment, and Application at Home, School, and in the Workplace* (pp. 343–362). San Francisco: Jossey-Bass.

Chopra, D., & Tanzi, R. E. (2012). *Super Brain: Unleashing the Explosive Power of Your Mind to Maximize Health, Happiness and Spiritual Well-Being*. New York: Random House.

Cooper, C. L., Cooper, R., & Eaker, L. (1988). *Living With Stress*. London: Penguin Books.

Cooper, C. L., Quick, J. C., & Schabracq, M. J. (Eds.). (2015). *International Handbook of Work and Health Psychology*. Chichester, UK: John Wiley & Sons.

Costa, G. (2003). Shift Work and Occupational Medicine: An Overview. *Occupational Medicine*, 53, 83–88.

Diener, E., & Larsen, R. J. (1993). The Experience of Emotional Well-Being. In M. Lewis & J. M. Haviland (Eds.), *Handbook of Emotions* (pp. 405–415). New York: Guilford.

Folkman, S., & Lazarus, R. S. (1991). Coping and Emotion. In A. Monat & R. S. Lazarus (Eds.), *Stress and Coping: An Anthology.* (pp. 207–227). New York: Columbia University Press.

Ford, M. T., Cerasoli, C. P., Higgins, J. A., & Decesare, A. L. (2011). Relationships Between Psychological, Physical, and Behavioural Health and Work Performance: A Review and Meta-Analysis. *Work and Stress*, 25, 185–204.

Fredrickson, B. L. (2000). Cultivating Positive Emotions to Optimize Health and Well-Being. *Prevention & Treatment*, 3, 1a.

Fredrickson, B. L. (2009). *Positivity: Top-Notch Research Reveals the Upward Spiral That Will Change Your Life*. New York: Harmony.

Gillin, J. C., & Byerley, W. F. (1990). The Diagnosis and Management of Insomnia. *New England Journal of Medicine*, 322, 239–248.

Goleman, D. (1995). *Emotional Intelligence*. New York: Bantam.

Goleman, D. (2000). Intelligent Leadership. *Executive Excellence*, 3, 17.

Health and Safety Executive. (2001). *Tackling Work Related Stress*. London: HSE Books.

Kabat-Zinn, J. (2012). *Mindfulness for Beginners: Reclaiming the Present Moment and Your Life*. Boulder, CO: Sounds True.

Kabat-Zinn, J., Lipworth, L., & Bruney, R. (1985). The Clinical Use of Mindfulness Meditation for the Self-Regulation of Chronic Pain. *Journal of Behavioral Medicine*, 8, 163–190.

Kabat-Zinn, J., Massion, A. O., Kristeller, J., Peterson, L. G., Fletcher, K. E., Pbert, L., Lenderking, W. R., & Santorelli, S. F. (1992). Effectiveness of a Meditation-Based Stress Reduction Program in the Treatment of Anxiety Disorders. *American Journal of Psychiatry*, 149, 936–943.

Kagan, A., & Levi, L. (1971). Adaptation of the Psychosocial Environment to Man's Abilities and Needs. In L. Levi (Ed.), *Society, Stress and Disease: The Psychosocial Environment and Psychosomatic Diseases*. London: Oxford University Press.

King, M. S., & D'Cruz, C. (2002). Transcendental Meditation, Hypertension and Heart Disease. *Aust Fam Physician*, 31, 164–168.

LaRocco, J. M., House, J. S., & French, J. R. Jr. (1980). Social Support, Occupational Stress, and Health. *Journal of Health and Social Behavior*, 21, 202–218.

Lazarus, R. S., & Folkman, S. (1984). *Stress, Appraisal and Coping*. New York: McGraw-Hill.

Maurer, R. (2004). *One Small Step Can Change Your Life: The Kaizen Way*. New York: Workman Publishing.

MBSR. (1979). Retrieved 8th November 2016: www.umassmed.edu/cfm/stress-reduction/history-of-mbsr/

Miller, G. (2009). Sleeping to Reset Overstimulated Synapses. *Science*, 324, 22–22.

Misra, S., & Stokols, D. (2012). Psychological and Health Outcomes of Perceived Information Overload. *Environment and Behavior*, 44, 737–759.

Moran, D. S., Eliyahu, U., Berlin, S., Hadad, E., & Heled, Y. (2007). Psychostimulants and Military Operations. *Military Medicine*, 172, 383–387.

Nieman, D. C. (1998). *The Exercise – Health Connection*. Champaign, IL: Human Kinetics Publishers.

Nyklicek, I., & Kuijpers, K. F. (2008). Effects of Mindfulness-Based Stress Reduction Intervention on Psychological Well-Being and Quality of Life: Is Increased Mindfulness Indeed the Mechanism? *Annals of Behavioral Medicine*, 35, 331–340.

Quick, J. C., Quick, J. D., Nelson, D. L., & Hurrell Jr, J. J. (1997). *Preventive Stress Management in Organizations*. Washington, DC: American Psychological Association.

Ross, A., & Thomas, S. (2010). The Health Benefits of Yoga and Exercise: A Review of Comparison Studies. *The Journal of Alternative and Complementary Medicine*, 16, 3–12.

Selye, H. (1956). *The Stress of Life*. New York: McGraw-Hill.

Slaski, M., & Cartwright, S. (2002). Health Performance and Emotional Intelligence: An Exploratory Study of Retail Managers. *Stress and Health*, 18, 63–69.

Straub, R. O. (2002). *Health Psychology*. New York: Worth Publications.

van Doornen, L. J., & De Geus, E. J. (1989). Aerobic Fitness and the Cardiovascular Response to Stress. *Psychophysiology*, 26, 17–28.

Yu, S., Yarnell, J. W. G., Sweetnam, P. M., & Murray, L. (2003). What Level of Physical Activity Protects Against Premature Cardiovascular Death? The Caerphilly Study, *Heart*, 89, 502–506.

8   Never give up! Keep advancing

Until now, we have introduced to you a lot of information and techniques, recognizing that such a plethora of new information cannot be easily assimilated at once. But as we said previously, this is normal, since change requires time and effort. Everything goes in relation to where you stand now in terms of your resilience levels and your overall lifestyle. Small daily actions will reinforce you to make a start and will work more effectively towards the development of your resilience than massive plans of action that will never be executed and will only make you feel guilty about yourself. Hence, set some realistic goals and start experimenting on any of the techniques that we have presented to you so far. Choose the ones that you like more. But you have to remember one thing. If you want to experience the results of being resilient, you need practice!

If you avoid practicing the aforementioned techniques that lead someone to become a resilient Spartan W@rker, it will make you eventually less able to cope with the everyday demands of your job/life and will also slow down your professional and personal development. The central idea underlying the philosophy behind the Spartan warriors is to never give up and keep on trying.

As the Spartans said, *i tan i epi tas*, which means that you return from a battle either with your shield or upon it.

There is not a right or wrong approach to the battle against stress and the route towards resilience. Everything depends on your current state. What are your current stress levels and how much do they affect your everyday life and overall wellbeing? At this point, we need to state that if your stress levels are high and overwhelming, you should consider the idea of undertaking a stress management training program that will help you alleviate in a short period of time some of the negative symptoms that you experience due to stress.

Stress management training programs

There are times in life when the levels of stress can be relatively high, thus disturbing our everyday function and making us feeling overwhelmed and unable to deal with that. Perhaps, it may be the case that the coping techniques that you are currently using are not enough and you need to extend your inventory of coping techniques in a more systematic way. In such cases, you should follow a more holistic and persistent approach against stress, with the assistance of a specialist on stress management, which should include a combination of the following (Cartwright & Whatmore, 2005):

- Stress awareness and education
- Relaxation techniques
- Cognitive coping strategies
- Biofeedback
- Meditation
- Exercise
- Lifestyle advice
- Interpersonal skills training.

The aim of such programs is to help individuals who experience increased discomfort to free themselves from the experience of such feelings and take control over their lives again. Sometimes life can be a burden, and we need some kind of support when we come to meet stressful situations and to reduce stress and its negative consequences. Of course, not everyone is an expert or, for example, not everyone has attempted to do meditation in the past, so training from a specialist will be needed at the beginning. A trap that you should avoid involves thinking that by following such a program you will manage stress for good. Well, this is inaccurate because stress research indicates that the effectiveness of such programs is limited due to the fact that they last for a short period of time. They usually give you a good boost and some basic guidelines for practicing on various techniques, but this is not enough, because if you stop practice, all the resulted benefits will gradually decay and you will return back to point zero (Bunce & West, 1996).

Alternatively, if you feel ready and highly motivated as you read this book, we advise you to extent your practicing level a step further by following our Spartan 6-day Bootcamp program. Following this 6-day program will really boost your efforts and your self-esteem, and it will also make you feel better, something that will motivate you in your future attempts as well. Consider this program as an induction training. Of course, you will have to show some discipline, but the more committed and engaged you become, the better the results for your own personal development would be.

The Spartan 6-day bootcamp

This is the beginning of a game-changing week for you. Throughout this week you are going to experience a number of new techniques. Most probably, you already know some of the techniques involved in the Spartan 6-day Bootcamp program, but it is the combination and intensity of this program that will offer new experiences to you. You will have to perform three exercises on a daily basis that will have a direct or indirect impact on your stress and resilience levels. The nature of some exercises will be lifestyle related, while the nature of others will be work related. You should be well organized throughout the process, so you will have to keep daily notes in your 'Spartan W@rker Diary'. A notebook divided into six sections (approximately four to five pages each, it depends on how much you like to write when you keep notes) is necessary. This program involves a diary week, from Monday to Saturday, so add a headline to each section starting from Agoge Day 1, Agoge Day 2 and so on (to refresh your memory, *agoge* is the Greek word for the Spartan upbringing and development system). You will have to be precise in the performance of your exercises because many of them will be present throughout the 6-day program, and hopefully they may become part of your new everyday behaviours and rituals. Each day will be divided as follows:

* Morning Spartan Reflection
* Spartan Act 1
* Spartan Act 2
* Spartan Act 3
* Spartan diary and planning.

Up to now, you have been informed of the Spartan philosophy of life and of all the scientific models and techniques that can transform your life. It is time to put this in practice, so let's begin with the first day of your new lifestyle. Keep in mind that you can adjust the Spartan Acts accordingly, based on your everyday schedule, since the current format of the program implies that you are occupied in a morning job. However, if you work in the afternoons or in swing shifts, you can adjust the activities accordingly, but once again you need to perform all of them.

Agoge Day 1

The first day and, particularly, the first morning of your change is considered as the most important time period of the whole program. Therefore, you must be well prepared for all the exercises of the day. If on the first morning you do not wake up feeling fully excited and motivated, then you are not ready yet for this program. The better you prepare yourself from the previous Sunday afternoon, the better your first day will flow. Have a look at your Spartan diary and reassure yourself that you have organized it properly. Then read all the exercises of the first day carefully and create an initial schedule of how you are going to perform them throughout your day. Make notes in your Spartan diary that will help you organize your day even better. Most probably this planning will take away any feelings of arousal, positive or negative, that you might experience due to the change in your everyday schedule that you are about to make. Having a clear picture of your future expectations will foster you to act better. A final hint is to try to sleep earlier than usual in order to wake up the following morning relaxed and refreshed.

Morning Spartan reflection

When you open your eyes, do not rush; try to stay at rest and reflect for a moment. Most people usually tend to rush throughout the day from the time they wake up until the time they go to bed again. Open your eyes, and instead of rushing, consider the following:

What are the five most important reasons that make you want to change your lifestyle? Take a few minutes to think about that, and be precise in your answers. When you are ready, stand up and write them down to your Spartan diary. Make raw notes and do not invest time to write things formally, since this is not important. The important thing for you is to become aware of your motives and of your purposefulness for doing all this.

The first thing that you should do every morning when you wake up is to drink a glass of fresh water. Your body has become dehydrated during sleep and is still under a relaxed phase. A glass of water will trigger all the functions of your internal organs. As discussed in Chapter 7, you should not pressure yourself to consume large quantities of water throughout the day, but of course you need to keep your organism hydrated, so four glasses of water throughout the day would be at least an appropriate minimum of daily consumption (morning, midday, afternoon and before you go to sleep). Decide when you want to do this by yourself during the day and set a reminder in your phone or an alarm in your watch. You will have to perform this act daily throughout the 6-day program. Committing to do so will help in the creation of your first new habit towards wellness.

Spartan Act 1

Since it is your first day, many thoughts might pass across your mind. Put on something comfortable and go for a 20-minute morning walk. If you have a pet, take your pet with you. It does not matter if this is a habit that you already have or not, the different thing here underlies the nature of your thoughts during such a walk. An important notice here is to leave your mobile phone at home. The purpose of this act is to keep your mind and focus away from your demanding daily schedule. This should be a mindful walk, where you fully experience the 'here and now' moment. Whether you walk in nature or in an urban environment does not matter; you can find beauty and interest in everything. If you have a pet, play with it, since pets can take the stress away just by shifting your focus of attention on them. When you return back home, take a warm shower, get ready slowly and, when ready, start your way to work.

Spartan Act 2

When you arrive at your office, think for a while how you run your work day, usually. Most likely you have specific rituals that you tend to follow, from how you process your emails and your workload to the way you structure/organize your meetings. By doing so, you might conclude that you are doing exactly the same things every day following the same sequence of events. In a way you run everything on autopilot, but how does this work for you? If you are feeling somehow stressed at work, you need to reschedule your routine to take control over the situation and your work life.

*   Set your phone on silent mode along with any notification that you receive from your laptop (i.e. emails, social media). In the beginning, you might feel somehow weird, but believe us, you have just saved yourself from information overload, a major occupational stressor.
*   Choose two 20-minute periods to check your emails throughout your work day. These periods might be in the morning and in the afternoon, one hour before you leave the office. Process only the emails that require no more than 2 minutes so as to take them out of the way; highlight the rest and let them be for the time being. Delete any unimportant emails at once.
*   Create a to-do list and prioritize the tasks that you have to do (include also highlighted emails). Classify them as 'urgent', 'important' and 'less important'.
*   Each individual experiences different periods of increased productivity within the working day. For some, such periods may occur during the

morning or during the early afternoon. When your productivity is at its peak, focus on the urgent matters.

- Isolate yourself. If you are in an open work space, wear headphones and put on some white-noise lounge music. The good thing when wearing the headphones (even if you do not listen to music) is that you will not get distracted by others. This technique will help you to become deeply engaged in your work and to manage big chunks of urgent work faster.
- When your productivity levels are much lower, for instance after your lunch break, it will be a better idea to schedule those meetings that you consider boring and occupy yourself with those tasks that require less cognitive effort to be done.

By intervening in your work schedule in such a way, eliminating distractions and negative multitasking, you will increase your productivity to a great extent, thus feeling more relaxed and less anxious because you have managed to address many of your urgent work matters successfully. It is of paramount importance to switch your mindset and leave all work matters behind when leaving the office. This technique needs practice, but you have at your disposition all the time needed to implement it. Keep on practicing it during the entire week.

Note: Do not forget to drink a glass of water in the specific times that you have set.

Spartan Act 3

Nutrition is very important for your health and bodily functions. There are two types of individuals: the ones who love cooking and the ones who hate it. It is not important which type you belong to; what is important is the quality of the foods that you tend to consume as well as the process of cooking and eating itself. As you leave the office, make a stop in the supermarket and spend some time buying the necessary ingredients for preparing your meals. Get lost in the corridors and in the scents of the supermarket and mindfully experience the act of being present moment by moment. We know that as you read this, the night before, the first thought that comes in your mind is that you do not have time. We agree, especially if you are not an experienced cook. However, there are several solutions to that. First of all, involve others in this act (family, spouse and/or friends) who can make this activity more exciting and fun. View such a process as a social activity that will bring you closer to others and will help to become more easily detached from your work. Second, decide from the previous day the menu of the next day and make a list of ingredients (this will save you time and money and also will discourage you from buying any unhealthy food). You can easily find a number of healthy recipes on the web that require 30–40 minutes and include starters, salads and main dishes in order to counteract the assumption of not having enough time. To conclude, dedicate some of your afternoon time to cooking and enjoy a high-quality dinner, but the purpose of this act is to do everything slowly. Do your shopping unhurried, cook slowly and most importantly eat slowly, experiencing each moment in detail. At the end, your energy deposits and resources will be replenished, you will feel satisfied with yourself since you have managed to eat a much healthier meal and, most importantly, you have released all the tension arising from your work, reducing your stress levels. Remember that being socially active and building meaningful social networks can enhance your overall wellbeing and resilience.

Note: Aim to cook another healthy dinner during the weekdays. We recognize the fact that this may be difficult for some of you, especially if you have a full schedule, but you should try to do so definitely on Saturday (Agoge Day 6), since you will probably not work and you will have the time to better experience the benefits of mindfully cooking and eating.

Spartan diary and planning

The end of each Agoge Day is very important for you because you need to reflect on the day that has passed and to become prepared for the following one. Reflection and planning are considered crucial because they shape your thoughts and consequently your actions, thus calming you down, especially when there are many things going on and your obligations are endless. Without planning, you will experience the chaos. The Spartan W@rker aims to be always one step ahead because this enables him/her to exert some control over life events. The experience of being able to exert some control over things dramatically reduces stress levels and boosts your self-esteem and self-confidence throughout the day.

Take a few minutes to reflect on your day, what went well and what you could have done better. Remember, there is no right or wrong way in your effort to become more resilient in life, it is just a trial-and-error process, with the aim to improve yourself and your techniques. Hence, write down in your Spartan diary all the actions that you performed throughout the day and how they made you feel. Try to use words like relaxed, satisfied, happy, cheerful or even stressed, discomfort etc. It is ok to feel somehow stressed and out of your comfort zone when you are trying to change things in your life. However, such negative emotions will be replaced with positive ones in a while. Some exercises may require writing your thoughts right away; the rest you will have to write down when you have concluded your day. Then reward yourself for the good job you did (e.g. reward yourself with a small portion of a healthy dessert or a glass of red wine) and start planning your next day by reading the exercises of the next Agoge Day.

Throughout the program, we invite you to try and go to sleep one hour earlier from the time you usually do. This will enable you to wake up the next day more relaxed and somewhat earlier in order to be able to perform your morning activities without hurrying. Remember that being able to wake up early will be a gift for you, since during the early morning hours distractions are minimal and you can dedicate some time to yourself, starting your day in the best possible way. Win the 'battle of the bed', because if you begin your day well, then most probably the rest of the day will also be a good one.

Note: The reading volume underlying the activities of the first day was extensive, but this happened intentionally to induct you properly into the process. The material presented in the next Agoge days will be more concise and summarised.

Excellent job; you have completed Agoge Day 1!

Agoge Day 2

Have a good day and keep up the good job.

Morning Spartan reflection

We human beings are very complex in the ways we function. The obligations that we have in our everyday lives tend to increase as we become older, making things even more complex. We human beings tend to forget the good things that exist in our lives, focusing only on the negative ones and on the ones that we do not have and we strive to achieve. The day that you will start feeling grateful for what you have in life is today. The Spartan W@rker prefers to live and experience life in modesty, appreciating what he/she actually has without being distracted from meaningless concerns, since he/she understands that in life there are both good and bad days. Allocate 5 minutes of your time and answer the following questions in your Spartan Diary:

1   Bring in your mind any negative concern that bothers you lately.
2   Write down any emotions related to your problem. Try not to withhold them even if such emotions create discomfort for you.
3   Now as you experience these emotions, think of five things in your life for which you are grateful and write them down. Two of them should be related to your actual problem and the other three to your life in general. An example concerning the problematic situation could be, 'I cannot

afford to pay all my monthly bills, but I am grateful because I have the skills to claim a promotion in my job and also because I have people in my life who support me in difficult times.'

4   Close your eyes and focus on the things that you are grateful for. Let your mind travel in these grateful thoughts, and other grateful thoughts soon will come to the surface, attracting positivism in your mind.

5   Take some moments to notice how you feel, how positive thoughts do create a positive sensation in your body and mind. Everything is within you, and you have the power to control your thoughts and your emotions. When you are ready, open your eyes and begin your day.

Whenever you feel down due to a problem, perform this exercise. It will only take 5 minutes of your time and will make you feel better and more motivated!

Spartan Act 1

Today your first action will be performed while you are going to work. It does not matter if you drive your car/motorbike/bike, walk to your work or take a bus/metro. This time period is very important and can affect your mood for the rest of the day, especially if you need, let's say, about 45 minutes to get to work. Wherever you are, try to focus on the moment and stop thinking of the things that may happen throughout the day. One good tip of advice is to break up the entire day into more manageable pieces, since this may help you to control things better and not to become overwhelmed by obligations. Most of us go to work in an autopilot mode. Sometimes we reach work without being consciously aware of how we did that, being lost in our running thoughts and increasing our levels of tension. Today, you will try to drive as you did it when you were learning driving for first time. Feel the steering wheel in your hands, be focused on how the car reacts whenever you change gear, how the tires touch the ground, how the air comes through the window. Be aware of the moments and concentrate on what is happening around you. Believe us, you will see and notice things that you have never noticed before. Try to breathe regularly and feel grateful for this morning activity. Your objective here is to be present, relaxed and focused, without becoming aroused by the possible traffic jam and the people around you who are in a constant rush. Controlling how you experience the morning route towards your work means to control your feelings during the rest of your day, which will definitely slow down your pace. Imagine being agitated even before entering your office, and then an emergency happens in the office that makes you explode. No one wants that.

Spartan Act 2

Although the majority of the exercises presented so far are relatively easy and not time-consuming, they require some time and discipline to be performed adequately. So, during this week you will attempt to leave earlier from work. Not earlier than you should, but on time! If, for example, you work from 9:00 am to 5:00 pm, then you would seek to have all your work done at 5:00. You will also try not to take work home. This might seem impossible in the beginning, but if you follow the work schedule that we discussed in Agoge Day 1, at 5:00 you will have managed to finish all emergency tasks/deadlines, and we are sure that you could postpone the rest for the next day. Keep in mind to prepare an action plan for the following work day before you leave the office. Such an action does not mean that you are not taking your work seriously. If you think about it, in the long run it will make you feel more productive, since you will have more time to defuse yourself and to calm down in the afternoons. With this technique, you will gain more free time to perform this week's exercises and also gain some time to spend with your friends and your loved ones.

Spartan Act 3

Today the third objective consists of adding some physical exercise in your schedule. You can freely choose any of the activities pertaining to physical exercise that we presented in the previous chapter. Based on your current levels of exercise, choose what you want to do: take a long walk, go to the gym or perform an outdoor activity or any kind of sport. Forty-five minutes to an hour will be sufficient. It would be even more beneficial for you if you decide to do physical exercise immediately after work, so prepare your exercise gear in the morning before you leave home. It would be easier for you to pass through the door of the gym if you have the exercise gear with you instead of returning back home to get it. When you finish the exercise, spend a moment to check on how you feel:

- Do you feel more energized and relaxed?
- Does your work or everyday problems seem less important?
- Do you feel more satisfied with yourself?

Most probably you will experience some or all of those things, and this happens because your endorphin and dopamine levels have been increased through physical activity, thus making you feel more relaxed and happier! Follow up with the rest of your day doing whatever you feel like! It would be beneficial for you to do some form of physical exercise again during the weekdays. If you cannot manage that, keep in mind that you will have to do so during Agoge Day 6 (Saturday), where you will have more free time available.

Note: Do not forget to drink water throughout the day. When you perform physical exercise, try to drink some more water during and after the exercise. Try to consume five glasses of water instead of four in the days that you do physical exercise. Always keep yourself hydrated. A good tip is to have a bottle of water and to sign the bottle with a marker in four segments (four glasses of water). This will make you follow up more easily.

Spartan diary and planning

Having finished your day and before completing your Spartan diary, choose a quiet area and perform a breathing exercise like the one we presented to you in Chapter 7 under the breathing techniques subsection. This exercise will help you to relax and to remain concentrated while writing your journal and planning your next day. When done, start reflecting on your day and feel proud of the things you have achieved. You have covered all your obligations, and in addition you have dedicated some time to yourself, doing beneficial things. Well done!

Plan your next day and have a nice evening! Do not forget to sleep earlier. Tomorrow is a new challenging day!

Agoge Day 3

The third day of your practice will include your efforts of being mindful as much as possible throughout the day. Being mindful will bring calmness and peacefulness to you.

Morning Spartan reflection

When you wake up in the morning, stay with your eyes closed for some minutes and perform again the same breathing exercise that you did the previous night. Check how much easier is for you to perform the exercise when you are relaxed in your bed. If any negative thought starts to emerge, do not become annoyed or judgmental toward yourself. Just accept that for the moment and bring your attention back to your breath, counting from 1 to 4 while you are inhaling and exhaling. Soon the fresh air that comes into your lungs will slowly send away the negative thoughts, along with the warm air that you exhale.

Spartan Act 1

Stand up and go to the kitchen. Drink a glass of water and observe the sensations that spring out as the water flows within your body like a waterfall, stimulating all of your internal organs. It is time to enjoy a mindful break-fast. Within the morning quiet, put some white-noise relaxing music playing in the background and slowly prepare your morning breakfast. Breakfast is considered the most important meal of the day. It will provide to your body all the needed nutrients and will boost your energy levels. It will also help you to avoid consuming any unhealthy snacks when you are at work. Make some eggs for protein, a piece of toast with slices of cheese and turkey, some fresh juice and your aromatic coffee or tea. The choices are many, but your choices have to be healthy. Be present by using all your senses while you prepare your breakfast. Smell, touch, hear and finally taste what you have created. Reward yourself and your body with a beautiful breakfast, and in turn they will reward you with a beautiful day.

Spartan Act 2

This morning ritual of eating breakfast will accompany you during your workday, where you might notice that you have completed your work tasks with more calm and attention. It is now midday, and is time to reboot your mindful attitude.

Either in your office or in a quiet area or outdoors during your lunch break, allocate 10–15 minutes to do some mindful guided meditation. You will need to wear your headphones for this exercise. Check on the web and locate a short guided meditation audio or video for stress reduction and relaxation. Sit in a comfortable position and close your eyes. We suggest a guided meditation, because while you are listening to a relaxing form of music, a voice will guide you to perform some actions, with the aim to relax you. This makes it easier for you to perform the meditation. The more expe-rienced you are in meditation, the more capable you become of mindfully meditating without anyone's guidance. This needs some practice, though. Perform a 10-minute meditation based on the instructions provided, and you will feel even more relaxed and satisfied with yourself. Your brain will not feel the presence of a wild horse jumping from one thought to another. You will perceive yourself being in a state of balance.

Well done! The rest of your working day will be easier to handle.

Spartan Act 3

You have two choices to follow after work: either attend a yoga session or go for a walk alone in nature, then perform some stretching exercises. It is up to you on what makes you feel more comfortable. The results will be the same: Relaxation and calmness. If you decide to do yoga, you will follow the flow and the instructions given from the yoga instructor, regardless of your experience level. As we discussed in the previous chapter, the benefits of yoga are many.

If you decide to go for a walk in nature, you have many alternatives (a park, a mountain, a lake or a beach), depending of course on where you live and what is nearest to you. Take a 30-minute walk and enjoy every single detail surrounding such walk: the noises, the scents and the view! Breathe deeply and connect with the nature around you. This will help you relax your mind during the busyness of the day. Walking in nature also gives you space to perceive and think about things in life from a different perspective. Keep in mind that Newton perceived the law of gravity while he was sitting under an apple tree and not while he was working in the laboratory. Observe the nature around you, lie on the ground and look at the sky, the birds and the clouds. . . . Connect with the moment.

Then you should perform some stretching exercises that will help you further relax both physically and mentally by releasing muscular tension and stress and by enhancing body and present moment awareness. Some guidelines for stretching are the following:

- Stretch for a period of 10–15 minutes.
- Stretch all parts of your body, starting from the upper part of your body, following with the lower part of your body and finishing with stretching your lower back.
- Hold each stretch position for 15–30 seconds, breathing deeply and focusing only on the muscles involved in each position.
- Always maintain a controlled movement during stretching and keep deepening the stretch gradually.
- You should never feel pain during stretching. If that is the case, it means that you are going too deep, so be careful and avoid injury.

Well done; your mindful day is finished. Enjoy an amazing afternoon!

Spartan diary and planning

Reflect on your day and write down your experiences. How was it, trying to be present in every moment of your day? Did you find it easy, or was it difficult to focus on the present moment? Did it make you feel stressed? Whatever the emotions experienced, positive or negative, it's OK. Change sometimes brings discomfort, especially if you tend to get lost in your thoughts and in your everyday obligations without experiencing what is happening in between. By doing so, you miss the journey of the day and you isolate yourself from others. Following such a mindful approach will defuse the stress before you return home and will make you feel ready to continue your day with your loved ones. Keeping yourself calm and positive will make you even more capable of confronting stressful situations in your everyday life successfully, and it will gradually boost your resilience levels. Write down everything in detail. Well done for taking care of yourself today; keep up the good work!

Now allocate some time to organize a plan for your next day. Reward yourself by eating a healthy snack before you go to sleep or by watching one of your favourite movies.

Agoge Day 4

As you read this paragraph, you are over the half-way mark for completing the Spartan 6-day Bootcamp. You have done a great job so far, so we would like you to begin your day by reflecting on your progress and the things that you have accomplished in only few days.

Morning Spartan reflection

As you wake up, try to recall how your lifestyle used to be a week ago and how many changes and attempts you have made to experience new things and to learn new stimulating ways that can help in your battle against stress and in becoming more mentally tough and resilient. Take a moment and ask yourself the following questions. Write down your answers in your Spartan diary:

1   How do I feel about myself during these days? Am I excited, or do I drag myself through the day?
2   Have my energy levels increased?
3   Do I feel satisfied with my performance at work and in my relationships with others?
4   Have my stress levels decreased at all?
5   How will my life be if I continue this program, let's say, for four consecutive weeks?

Take some time to reflect on your answers. For instance, if you are bored and you drag yourself through the process, what might be the cause? Usually, boredom can be a sign of avoiding something, something that we feel uncomfortable with. But this is OK, and it is usually part of the process when we attempt to modify our habits. As we have stated a number of times throughout this book, change needs time and effort.

Spartan Act 1

As we have already mentioned, in order to change and improve overall wellbeing, you need to take some action. Even small actions can enhance your wellbeing, and it is the accumulation of these small actions that in the long run will transform you completely into a new person. So today you are going to implement new changes throughout your day. If you do not usually eat breakfast (something that we tried to change yesterday), have a healthy breakfast, and your overall performance will be improved throughout your day. Use a different route to go to work and on your way back home and you will be distracted from negative thoughts because you will shift your focus on new surroundings, and that will get you out of autopilot mode. Reduce your intake of caffeine and replace it with green tea, lemon water or fresh juices, and you will save yourself from the experience of pseudo stressor factors and negative arousal and tension throughout your workday. Take regular breaks when you are at work (10 minutes every hour) and you will improve the ways through which you handle difficult situations and demanding projects at work. Rearrange your office space, clean and remove any unnecessary elements that will only distract you. Keep only what is needed; save yourself from hassles and improve your productivity levels. Avoid taking any work home (do so only if there is a real emergency, but again stop working at least one hour before you go to sleep) and dramatically reduce your stress levels by having more personal time to recover and replenish your resources for the next day. Finally, take it slowly no matter what you do: eat slowly, speak slowly, walk slowly, think slowly and breath slowly. Slow down your pace and be peaceful. The list is endless, so follow our examples, and also add things you like that will make your day cheerful and satisfying.

Spartan Act 2

Expand your work social network and your social network in general. Until now, we have pointed out the significance of social support both in the battle against stress and in the process of becoming more resilient. Your second action for today will be to enrich your existing relationships as well as to create new ones both at work and in your personal life. In terms of work, instead of talking only about work-related issues, enrich your discussions with social chats. As we said in Chapter 7, show that you care, be loyal and helpful towards others. This will not take much time from your work and it will not distract others, either;, it will more likely be a positive break for them. Instead of sending multiple impersonal emails, go to your colleague's desk (you will also do some walking) and have a short face-to-face conversation. This will create a stronger bond between both of you. In your personal life, start contacting your friends through the phone or through social media on a regular basis and arrange frequent gatherings and meetings when it is possible. Listen to their concerns and show them that you are there for them. Also expand your social network by meeting new people with whom you can relate based on common interests (business, sports, hobbies etc.). Most importantly, whether you are married or not, dedicate meaningful time to your spouse and family in general. Plan common activities and add some romance in your everyday structured life. Always remember that we are human beings and not 'human doings', and human beings are genetically programmed to interact with others and be socially active. This brings peacefulness, reduces our stress levels and makes us better able to cope during difficult times.

Spartan Act 3

During your afternoon hours, we would like you to consider the following question: Have you ever wondered what you really need for being happy? Well, the answer seems to be simpler than you might think. Spend some time to consider the activities that have given to you a sense of pleasure and happiness in the past, and just do more of them. Write down a list of things and actions in your Spartan diary and highlight them with a tick every time you perform one of them. The more the highlighted ticks, the better the results for you. This technique will be familiar to you, since we are discussing habits and behaviours that you have already performed in the past. Invest time in them and you will feel happier and more complete.

Spartan diary and planning

As you do every day, try to have a relaxing and pleasant afternoon. You can complete your Spartan diary and have a look at the acts of the following day whenever you want to. Plan your fifth Agoge Day and prepare yourself for the upcoming weekend.

You did a great job – congratulations!

Agoge Day 5

Morning Spartan reflection

Good day! Today's morning Spartan reflection is combined with Spartan Act I.

Spartan Act 1

Your first act today will involve what we call early morning ritual. We have already mentioned that but not in detail. Waking up early is one of the most significant factors toward personal and professional success. Something very special happens during the early morning hours, and the most special thing is that there is minimal distraction. Everyone (family, colleagues etc.) and everything is still sleeping, so during this time that you have created for yourself you can do those things that you have always been lamenting not having time to do. You have time to read, exercise, meditate, go for a morning walk, sit by yourself and enjoy in total silence a cup of coffee. Magical moments! When you will start creating such a new habit, it will be difficult in the beginning, so try gradually waking up earlier by 30 minutes at a time. The earlier you wake up, the better your day will flow. Also, by exercising in the morning you will go to work more relaxed and focused and you will have your afternoons free to do things that make you happy. So for the last working day of your week, try to wake up as much earlier as you can and perform any of the activities that we mentioned previously or anything that you might want in general.

Spartan Act 2

Never give up! Keep advancing!

You are a human being, and as a human you will make mistakes in life. The goal is to make mistakes, to fail but always to get on your feet again. Failure, although it hurts in the beginning and diminishes your self-esteem level, is not always bad for you. If you look at the bright side, you can learn through your failures and become more resilient in the future. Do not be afraid of failure; through taking risks and confronting your fears, you eventually improve your adaptability levels. Therefore, try to think of a recent situation where you have failed in something and proceed with elaborating on the following by writing down your answers in your Spartan diary:

- How did the failure make you feel? Describe your emotions.
- Now try to consider what you did that did not work that well and what you could have done better.
- Try to think which problem-solving techniques you could use in the future for dealing better with similar situations.
- Consider how you could control your emotional reactions better next time so as to reduce experienced stress levels.

Keep in mind that in order to develop your resilience you must take considerable risks in life, getting out of your comfort zone. So explore the world around you, accumulate more life experiences and find ways to adapt yourself better to change and uncontrollable situations. Through experience and persistence, you will improve significantly each aspect of your life.

Spartan Act 3

In this final act of the day, we are going to discuss the impact of worrying in life. Do you want to be a Spartan warrior or a 'Spartan worrier'? The modern lifestyle and the fast pace of life has made people to be in a constant rush, always worrying about things that are going to happen, without laughing and enjoying life. You need to understand that many of the things that you are worrying about never will happen, and the ones that will happen will definitely not happen today. So stop worrying and feeling guilty about what has happened in the past, and definitely stop worrying about what might happen in the future. The task of the day and for the forthcoming days of your life is to think of a specific hour during the day in which you can allow yourself to freely worry. Think of any problematic situation that preoccupies you, but after that time period you must try to carry on with your day, avoiding any negative thought until the next day. Live the present moment in your life, create beautiful moments and experiences for your loved ones and do it again the following day. Whatever might be a worry for you today, think whether you will remember it after two months. Was it so important after all? If the answer is no, then there is no need to trouble yourself. Calm down and think of a fun and pleasant activity that you can organize for this afternoon that will make you and those close to you to have a great time! In life, you should try to create as many beautiful moments as you can. After all, this is the meaning of life – to be positive and happy!

Spartan diary and planning

Spend some time reflecting on the whole week that passed. You really did a great job, and you demonstrated the discipline and commitment needed to become a Spartan W@rker. Keep on changing your lifestyle and experience the benefits in your overall wellbeing. Make notes in your Spartan diary and plan for the final Agoge day.

Agoge Day 6

The last day of your Spartan 6-day Bootcamp is a special day. There is no rush and there is no any fixed schedule for you. Just wake up whenever you want to without using an alarm clock, and praise yourself for the good job that you have done during the week. This day includes only two acts for you to perform. The first one involves physical exercise, and the second one involves mindful cooking. You have already performed both of them during the week (second and first Agoge days, respectively), and today you can further perform them in a more relaxed pace, since it is Saturday. Plan them as you like!

Furthermore, during the rest of the day we will assess how strongly you related to the acts that you performed throughout the week. Plan to do some of the techniques that you enjoyed the most during the Spartan Bootcamp. The more the better; it is up to you. Enjoy your day!

Spartan diary and planning

Before you go to bed, write down all your daily activities in the Spartan diary, and then reflect for a moment on the week that passed and on the effect that it had on you. Reflect on the following questions:

- Are you satisfied with the exercises and with the ways through which you have managed things?
- Was it easy for you, or was it very demanding?
- Would you do it again?
- Will you include any of the aforementioned activities in your everyday lifestyle from now on?
- Do you feel physically and/or mentally stronger?

Today there is no any planning to do, because tomorrow is Sunday. . . . You did an excellent job! Well done. Spend your Sunday by rewarding yourself for successfully following the program until the end. We hope that it did make a difference in your everyday life.

Summary

In this chapter, we presented a detailed 6-day program for you to practice based on the techniques that we have discussed in our previous chapters. As stated in the beginning of the chapter, although such short-term programs are beneficial and can alleviate some of the stress symptoms that you might experience, they do not have a permanent effect, and the practice of such coping techniques must be done regularly. We propose that you keep on acting like a Spartan W@rker for a couple of weeks, following the structure of the program presented in this chapter. This will strengthen your attitudes towards the adoption of healthier behaviours, making it easier to include them in your everyday life, thus creating a completely new lifestyle for you: a lifestyle based on wellbeing.

References

Bunce, D., & West, M. A. (1996). Stress Management and Innovation Interventions at Work. *Human Relations*, 49, 209–232.

Cartwright, S., & Whatmore, L. (2005). Stress and Individual Differences: Implications for Stress Management. In A. S. Antoniou & C. L. Cooper (Eds.), *A Research Companion to Organizational Health Psychology* (pp. 163–173). Cheltenham: Edward Elgar.

Epilogue, rescue mission
Help others become Spartan W@rkers

We believe that already you have an idea of what the Spartan W@rker concept is all about. We hope that you have found the material of this book inspiring, discovering useful tips that will lead to the improvement of an overall positive and resilient way of being.

Having completed the Spartan Bootcamp, we would not be surprised if we see you adopting the Spartan W@rker lifestyle that others around you, from loved ones to business colleagues, widely notice in you. Now it's time for you to become an exemplar for others! Now it's time for you to assist others' attempts in their way of change! There is no greater satisfaction than the one gained from helping other people, so at this point we recommend you pass your acquired knowledge to others and become the starting point of their change. Helping others will create in you a sense of accomplishment and internal satisfaction, since you will contribute to the improvement of their lifestyles to a great extent.

The world around us urgently needs more positive people, people who are happy and satisfied, people who experience the beauty in everything that they do. Passing on your experience can improve the lives of other people around you. It is a reciprocal interaction that will help you strengthen your motivation, self-confidence and self-worth while participating in the creation of a new Spartan W@rker who will rise along with you.

The act of helping others is central for the development of our communities, and by doing so we embrace a positive/humanistic approach. This is the remedy against negativity, toxicity and mediocrity in life. Unfortunately, we are surrounded by toxic and negative people, a category of individuals that can be easily found even among intimate friends and family. Although the Spartan W@rkers are emotionally intelligent enough so as not to be affected by the toxic and negative people surrounding them, they recognize how important it is to interact with positive people with whom they share the same mentality and points of view. So, motivate others around you! Take them with you for a walk in nature, ask them to participate in some of the exercises included in this book, talk to them, motivate them! Explain to them both the physical and psychological benefits that they would experience if they follow a healthier lifestyle. Work as a team!

The Spartans greatly supported the philosophy of teamwork, a term that we use widely nowadays both in the personal and in the working environment. The idea of doing things in a better way when we are all together instead of when we are alone is one that stimulates us. Living in a demanding society where competition is high acts as an inhibitor of teamwork. If we want to use one of the most important assets of the ancient Spartans, it would be that of implementing teamwork and team bonding in our lives. Encouraging others besides ourselves is a remarkable thing to do!

Let us not forget that the concept of this book was created by using as a paradigm the characteristics of a spectacular and unique population, namely the Spartans, blending them with the characteristics of our contemporary urban lives. It is so fascinating! However, it will be even more fascinating to witness an increase in your self-confidence and resilience when you attempt to apply the techniques proposed throughout this book in your daily life.

Perhaps, as you unfold the pages of this book, you will find some topics a little bit blurry or new to you. That should not discourage you in any way. As we repeatedly have mentioned, change needs time and effort. Practice and growth are ongoing processes. By neglecting practicing, you will not get the results that you wish to, so get your Spartan tools set, be motivated and organized, give yourself the opportunity to advance and be prepared for the 'battle'. All humans possess an internal strength that remains hidden until it becomes awakened. Awaken it by primarily believing in yourself. Have faith in your potential and capabilities, and you will be impressed by the results. It's always more difficult until it's done. Just start, and you will gain more confidence along the way as you gradually step out of your comfort zone.

Index

Printed in the United States
by Baker & Taylor Publisher Services